WHAT PEOPLE ARE SAYING ABOUT DANETTE JOY CRAWFORD AND *LIMITLESS THINKING, LIMITLESS LIVING*

Danette Crawford has displayed a life of *Limitless Thinking* and *Limitless Living* by impacting communities all over Hampton Roads and this nation. I've known Danette and have worked closely with her for many years. She doesn't just talk it—she walks it! Danette Crawford and her outreach ministry have played a vital role in not only reducing the crime rate, but also in changing the lives of youth and adults in low-income areas. She has worked closely with the police department, the mayor's office, and other city officials to bring life-altering changes in the most challenging areas of our city. Our police department has even tracked that the crime rate has been lowered significantly in the areas where she works. Danette Crawford has made a tremendous difference right here in Virginia Beach. As you read her book, *Limitless Thinking, Limitless Living*, I believe you will be inspired to walk in a limitless lifestyle that she demonstrates daily.

—*William D. Sessoms, Jr.*
Mayor, Virginia Beach, VA

Danette Crawford is a leader with a passion to "walk in the call" on her life and "seize the land" God has called her to take. She wants that for you, too! I love *Limitless Thinking, Limitless Living* because it is filled with the promises of God for those who love Him. Danette has done the legwork for us, pointing out the potential pitfalls and encouraging the paths to favor and provision. Read this book with a pencil in hand so you can underline all that God speaks to your heart as you learn to think and walk in the limitless promises of God.

—*Terry Meeuwsen*
Co-host, *The 700 Club*; founder, Orphan's Promise

D1111999

Danette Crawford is an exceptional leader who has used her principles of *Limitless Thinking, Limitless Living* to build a ministry that serves so many in need. She has lived out the principles in her book and that is the best testimony.

—*Dr. Ted Baehr*
Founder and publisher, *Movieguide*

Danette Crawford's book, *Limitless Thinking, Limitless Living*, is a must-read for anyone who desires to make a difference in the lives of those around them. It will also challenge you to believe beyond the ordinary and take radical steps of faith to reach your full potential. Life's opportunities never end, and her book and life will inspire you to make the most of the opportunities that God is putting in front of you.

Danette has been a personal friend of mine for many years. I have known Danette since the early days of my salvation as a teenager when I went into a little Pentecostal church where she was the youth pastor. She has always been a true champion of the faith. Regardless of what she has faced in life, her love for God and for His people has stayed consistent. No matter what season of life I have found myself in or that she herself has been in, she has always been a woman of great faith, character, and consistency. Danette is a living example of how faith can cause change in our lives and in the lives around us. It is because of her faith and obedience that she has impacted millions of lives through books, television, and compassion outreaches. It is my honor and privilege to endorse Danette's latest book, *Limitless Thinking, Limitless Living*.

—*Pastor Paula White-Cain*
Evangelist and senior pastor, New Destiny Christian Center,
Orlando, FL

Danette Crawford provides an in-depth, mind-bending, heartwarming, and soul-stirring account of how God always seeks to embrace us with his compassionate, eternal love. Whatever you did in your past, however you are living in the present, or wherever you imagine to be for a shipwrecked future, this book invites you to see life through a brighter vision. *Limitless Thinking, Limitless Living* reveals the biblical truths about God's unlimited blessings for those who seek him. Jesus said, *"Seek first the kingdom of God and all its righteousness and all things will be added unto you"* (Matthew 6:33). Therefore, open your mind, heart, and soul, and receive this timely message from Danette Crawford. Take the limits off God. Then follow his lead to remarkable hope and future of an abundant life. It's a new season!

—*Kelly Wright*
Owner, America's Hope News LLC; former anchor, Fox News Network

There will not be a valid excuse left to give up and quit after you read *Limitless Thinking, Limitless Living*, the latest book by Danette Crawford. If you have been struggling with your mission, your purpose, or your focus, let the words of this book inspire and teach you how to grab hold of your vision and see it explode with possibilities. The ancient prophet Habakkuk instructed us to "write the vision and make it plain that we can run with it." Danette's book shows you how to prepare, write, believe, and see it come to pass.

—*Garth and Tina Coonce*
Founders, TCT Network

Pastor Danette Crawford is a powerhouse in the Kingdom of God! Caring for the downtrodden, she has dedicated her life to encouraging, inspiring, and elevating all those she encounters. Filled with moving testimonies and insightful examples, *Limitless Thinking, Limitless Living* will help you pursue God's best for your life. As a spiritual covering to Pastor Danette, I know her greatest hope is to see others overcome their struggles and live abundantly. This book is the perfect first step for all of us.

—*Pastor Dan Willis*
Founder and senior pastor, The Lighthouse Church
of All Nations, Alsip, IL

Danette Crawford's new book, *Limitless Thinking, Limitless Living*, will challenge you to get out of your comfort zone and reach for your potential zone! It will show you, through practical Biblical steps, how to cross over to the next level in every area of your life. Whatever perceived limitations have been in your life, get ready to have victory over them. Your mindset will change and your launch forward will be successful as you learn how to think big, ask big, expect big, and receive BIG!

—*Pastor Tony Suarez*
Executive vice president, National Hispanic Christian
Leadership Conference

Limitless Thinking, Limitless Living will be a great encouragement and provide insight to anyone seeking God's direction for their life. We tend to think too small, limiting what we can accomplish in our lifetime even though we have been given the Holy Spirit as our Helper. The journey of walking with God is what every believer can experience. We all have a purpose in being here. I recommend *Limitless Thinking, Limitless Living* for your spiritual growth.

—*Dr. Bob Rodgers*
Senior pastor, Evangel World Prayer Center, Louisville, KY

I read every book Danette Crawford writes! Her life is proof God rewards those who are obedient and hungry. *Limitless Thinking, Limitless Living* will show you how to dream BIG, while sitting at the feet of the Holy Spirit. Danette is passionate about unlocking your unlimited future, with an unlimited God. Read this book and run into your future!

—*Dr. Mike Smalley*
President, Worldreach Ministries

In her book, *Limitless Thinking, Limitless Living*, Danette Crawford challenges, inspires, encourages, and instructs us to not settle for anything less than what God has intended for our lives. She makes it abundantly clear that the possibility for a "limitless" existence rests squarely in the reality of God's own *unlimited* ability! This book is not just a shallow exhortation for the reader to "think positive and think big." Rather, Danette is calling us back to becoming deeply rooted in the true revelation of God's unlimited power and ability. In this work, we are being called to become numbered among the Joshua generation, those brave hearts who are seeking to "cross over" the bounds of thinking and living that has been marked by certain limitations, fully enter into all God has planned for His dear children, and cross over and enter a life marked by a kingdom existence where the very notion of limitation doesn't even exist. Or as Paul wrote, *"Now unto Him that is able to do exceeding abundantly above all that we ask or think, according to the power that worketh in us"* (Ephesians 3:20 KJV).

—*Rev. Phil Cappuccio*
Prophet/teacher, Alexandria, VA

Once again, Danette Joy Crawford has blessed us with very wise counsel. *Limitless Thinking, Limitless Living* is probably the finest book I have ever read that combines the best of biblical and practical wisdom. It's not theoretical or secondhand advice, but tried and true wisdom that comes from her personal, victorious walk with the Lord. In short, it's a book about the Refiner's divine guidance that will keep its readers spiritually insulated throughout life's fiery trials.

—*William F. Cox, Jr., Ph.D.*
Professor, Christian Education Programs,
Regent University School of Education

LIMITLESS THINKING

THINK BIG, ASK BIG,
EXPECT BIG, AND RECEIVE BIG!

LIMITLESS LIVING

DANETTE J. CRAWFORD

WHITAKER
HOUSE

Limitless Thinking, Limitless Living
Think Big, Ask Big, Expect Big, and Receive Big!

Danette Joy Crawford
Danette Crawford Ministries
P.O. Box 65036
Virginia Beach, VA 23467
DanetteCrawford.com

ISBN: 978-1-64123-158-9 • eBook ISBN: 978-1-64123-159-6
Printed in the United States of America
© 2018 by Danette Joy Crawford

Whitaker House
1030 Hunt Valley Circle
New Kensington, PA 15068
www.whitakerhouse.com

Library of Congress Cataloging-in-Publication Data:
LC record available at https://lccn.loc.gov/2018025529

1 2 3 4 5 6 7 8 9 10 11 WH 25 24 23 22 21 20 19 18

CONTENTS

FOREWORD

This inspiring, well-researched book by my good friend and confident, Danette Crawford, is the blueprint we have all been searching for
throughout our lives.

Danette is not only a relevant author, but also an international evangelist, speaker, and a TV host with an encouraging message of hope.
She is the founder and president of Danette Crawford Ministries,
which aims to spread the gospel around the globe with its media endeavors. This powerful, anointed, positive, successful, and energetic lady is
also president of Joy Ministries Evangelistic Association, an "outreach"
arm that organizes inner-city work with over twenty different compassion programs. Danette has written this book out of her amazing

experiences and demonstrates how she has been able to accomplish an abundance of winning success in her life.

The insights contained in this book can change your circumstances and guide you through the process of finding *Limitless Thinking* and obtaining the *Limitless Living* we all desire.

I am a result of the principles applied in this book! I have been healed of multiple myeloma cancer. I am now happily married and continue to have a successful career as a touring Christian recording artist.

Is there something missing in your life? Are you just letting life happen to you? Maybe you have given up hope on your dreams. Do you know what God really thinks of you, wants for you, and has provided for you? Do you know why you're not experiencing it?

Await no longer—your answers are here! Don't put this book down, my friend. You will find the answers to these questions and many more as you travel through the incredible journey of *Limitless Thinking, Limitless Living.*

—*Carman Domenic Licciardello*
Carman World Outreach

INTRODUCTION: GET READY FOR THE CROSSOVER!

At Joy Ministries, our staff meets every Monday for an extended session of corporate prayer, during which we join together to seek the Lord's blessing and direction for the week ahead. I love these sessions, during which the Lord often speaks to me in life-changing ways. When I'm on the road, I deeply regret having to miss staff prayer. It's a time of glorious visitation from the Lord and it offers a chance to bond, unify, and strengthen ourselves as a ministry staff.

At one particular prayer session, God said to me, "Moses is dead." That statement really shook me. I immediately knew in my spirit that someone was going to die. I had no idea who, how, or when, but it was clear God was informing me of someone's impending death.

I remained with my staff for about two hours, until our prayer time concluded. By the end of the session, I had received a few more details regarding God's statement, yet I still didn't know who was going to die or when. Each time God speaks to us in a manner that is vague, I believe He wants us to seek His face continually, until He shares with us the full details of His instructions and reveals the complete meaning of the things He has spoken to us. In this case, all I knew was God was telling me I needed to get ready to lead at a whole different level. God showed me, during those two hours, that I had been poured into, trained, and equipped. And now it was time for me to step forward and lead at a higher level.

Several months later, the assistant pastor of my first church went home to be with the Lord. She was a great woman of God and the Lord had used her mightily to start the church I had attended for many years—the church where I was first trained for ministry. As soon as I heard she had gone to be with the Lord, I knew this was what the Lord had been speaking about the day He'd said to me, "Moses is dead."

What I didn't know was that several major national leaders would also die over the next several years. As I heard about one great leader after another who had gone to be with the Lord, God kept whispering in my ear, "This is what I was speaking to you about." These were the leaders who had trained, equipped, and led the people of my generation. God was saying, "They have completed their course; now, you, and all the people of this generation, *get ready!*"

THE SEASON OF "GET READY"

Many of us are in the season of "get ready." Usually, when God tells us, "Get ready," it doesn't mean something big is going to happen in the next twenty-four hours. It doesn't necessarily mean something is going to happen in the next six months either. It means only that we must submit to God and embrace the season of "get ready," or we won't *be* ready when the time God has appointed does arrive.

In the season of "get ready," we may feel we've been overlooked, forgotten, or even abandoned. I want to encourage you today: you haven't been overlooked; actually, you have been chosen—and that's why God is getting you ready. He's getting you ready for your crossover. He's getting you ready for your "suddenly." He's getting you ready for your promotion, your new season, your total turnaround. If you don't go through the process of getting ready, you won't be ready when your "suddenly" does arrive. *Suddenly*, you'll be called out of the season of "get ready" and summoned into your season of blessing and promotion. *Suddenly*, you will be ushered into the next level. Being fully ready is an important key.

> IN THE SEASON OF "GET READY," WE MAY FEEL WE'VE BEEN OVERLOOKED, FORGOTTEN, OR EVEN ABANDONED.

The book of Joshua opens with God commanding Joshua to get ready to cross the Jordan River and claim the land He was about to give to His people, the Israelites.

> *After the death of Moses the servant of the LORD, the LORD said to Joshua son of Nun, Moses' aide: "Moses my servant is dead. Now then, you and all these people, get ready to cross the Jordan River into the land I am about to give to them—to the Israelites."*
>
> (Joshua 1:1–2)

Whenever God is about to give you something—whenever God is about to bless you, promote you, or exalt you—you must *get ready* for it.

SEASONS OF LIFE

We often think of seasons as a certain time of year, such as the spring, a rainy season, or the Christmas season. But a season can also be a time "characterized by a particular circumstance or feature."

God plans and permits various seasons in our lives so we may develop our character and grow our faith, ever advancing in our walk with Him. There are seasons of flourishing and seasons of failure. There are seasons of growth and seasons of gathering the fruits of that growth. And each season is intended to fully prepare and equip us for the season that will follow it.

I can say without a doubt that God has ordained the length and timing of each season of my life. I may kick and scream, I may complain and whine, about a season I don't like, but none of that will bring the unpleasant season to an end any quicker. On the contrary, I've found that those types of negative reactions actually prolong the duration of unpleasant seasons. The children of Israel spent forty years whining and complaining as they wandered around in the wilderness, waiting to reach the Promised Land. And we may catch ourselves doing the same thing if we aren't careful.

The Israelites' season of crossing over into the Promised Land should have only taken eleven days. But as a group, they were stubborn, self-centered, and unfocused. Thus, their whining continued and most of them died in the wilderness without ever reaching the Promised Land. When we maintain a good attitude, when we focus on our blessings instead of our problems, we can praise our way through any unpleasant season and be ready for the next one.

SEASONS ARE PERSONAL

In the season of "get ready," God wants to do a great work within us. This desired work varies according to each person's needs and the assignment God has in mind. We should never compare our own season of preparation with someone else's. We never know what that person may have gone through in order to prepare for the place where God has promoted him. It may seem to us that he just popped up overnight, but we are likely clueless about all the preparations he has endured and the price he has paid to attain that promotion.

Have you ever known someone who seemed to zip straight to the top? Maybe you worked hard for ten years, hoping for a promotion, only to watch as the new "kid on the block" landed that very position in an instant. Don't worry—and especially don't get in the middle of God's business. Keep your heart right and your mouth shut as you remember that all promotion comes from the Lord, who raises up one, but brings down another. (See Psalm 75:6–7.)

SEASONS ARE STRATEGIC

Part of your season of "get ready" may be a test of how you will react and respond to the new kid on the block getting the position you desired. God's eye is ever upon us and He cares greatly about the way we react to others' blessings and promotions. A bad attitude and an envious heart could be the very things that disqualify us for a promotion. Such a heart attitude, when discovered, might suggest we aren't as "ready" as we thought we were.

> PART OF YOUR SEASON OF "GET READY" MAY BE A TEST OF HOW YOU WILL REACT AND RESPOND.

It amazes me how God loves us so much that He prepares us and gets us ready, no matter how much junk or baggage we need to work through. If we will only let Him, He will use our hardships and challenges to prepare us for the high places He has in store for us. God is always getting us ready for our next season. Always remember, whatever you are going through today, it's only temporary. Soon enough, the season of "get ready" shall pass and you will stand victorious on the other side.

GET READY...FOR WHAT?

God commanded Joshua and the children of Israel to get ready and then He showed them what it was they were getting ready for. He wanted them to get ready for something *big*!

Here is what He said to Joshua:

I will give you every place where you set your foot, as I promised Moses. Your territory will extend from the desert to Lebanon, and from the great river, the Euphrates—all the Hittite country—to the Mediterranean Sea in the west. No one will be able to stand against you all the days of your life. As I was with Moses, so I will be with you; I will never leave you nor forsake you. Be strong and coura- geous, because you will lead these people to inherit the land I swore to their ancestors to give them. (Joshua 1:3–6)

God was asking Joshua to think big. He was trying to get him to think outside the box, to reach far beyond the confines of his comfort zone. God described the land He had in store for the Israelites as exten- sive. In other words, He was saying, "I have *big stuff* in store for you."

We seem to have an easier time believing God has "big things" planned for other people than to imagine He has big things and boun- tiful blessings for us. Why is that? Usually, it's a result of our limited thinking. When we have limited thinking, we live with self-imposed confines on the capabilities of ourselves, of God, and of others. We limit God. We limit ourselves. We limit our own potential.

In Joshua 1:3–6, God challenged Joshua's thinking because He wanted him—and the people he would lead—to live without limits. God wants us to live without limits, too. He wants us to take our own land and possess all of the promises He has in store for us. In order for us to do that, we must get ready and be prepared. A major part of the process of getting ready is developing what I call "limitless thinking." Only when we have limitless thinking can we qualify for limitless living.

The purpose of this book is to expand your thinking, enlarge your vision, and increase your expectations of what God can and *will* do in you, through you, and for you. There's a life of limitless power and potential just waiting to be unleashed within you, if you'll only learn to think the way God does and live the way He asks us to.

All around, we encounter limits. Some of them are physical, others are mental; some of them are imposed by other people and society, others are imposed by our own thinking and behavior. By the power of the Holy Spirit, we can push past these limits and overcome all obstacles to the glorious life of limitless potential God has planned for us. Are you ready to cross over to the next level? Get ready—your life without limits is about to begin!

PART I:

PREPARE TO CROSS OVER

1

GETTING READY—
A PERSONAL PROCESS

I've learned an important key to being ready as I continually await the next season that God has for me. I say "continually" because as soon as one season changes, God is already preparing us and getting us ready for the *next* season. This is a process that will continue until we get to heaven. God takes us from glory to glory, from level to level. (See 2 Corinthians 3:18.) It's a limitless process, so don't limit God and don't limit yourself.

When we finally reach the next level or the next season, we shouldn't camp out there and retire just because we feel fulfilled, content, or even exhausted. Yes, we should enjoy the new season and embrace the new level. But we haven't seen anything yet! There's still a lot more that God has for us.

We must not "retire" before we've fulfilled our God-given potential, which is only as big as our thinking. "Reach for the moon and at least land on the stars," as Bishop John Gimenez used to say to me. When I was going through various trials in ministry, he would say, "Oh, Danettie, you are just going through your necessaries." Those "necessaries" weren't fun. Trials and tribulations rarely are. But they were a necessary part of my getting ready for all that God had ahead for me.

Maybe today, you are going through your "necessaries." If so, rejoice! You are being made ready for all that the Lord has ahead for you.

BE READY WHEN GOD NEEDS YOU

God spoke to the prophet Jeremiah with these words of exhortation: "*Get yourself ready! Stand up and say to them whatever I command you. Do not be terrified by them, or I will terrify you before them*" (Jeremiah 1:17). Once, when I read that verse, the Holy Spirit said to me, "Too many people spend all their time trying to get others ready and, as a result, they themselves are not ready when I need them."

Did you know that God has need of you? He sure does! He has exciting projects planned for you. Ephesians 2:10 says, "*For we are God's workmanship, created in Christ Jesus to do good works, which God prepared in advance for us to do.*" And no one else can do those works like you can. As a minister, I am equipped and able to reach certain people who otherwise wouldn't hear the gospel or receive the help and guidance they need. You, too, have the ability and the skills to assist, serve, and otherwise help certain people whom I could never reach for the Lord.

God has prepared you, created you, and called you to do specific things for Him

> GOD HAS PREPARED YOU, CREATED YOU, AND CALLED YOU TO DO SPECIFIC THINGS FOR HIM NO ONE ELSE CAN DO.

no one else can do. There are works He has prepared in advance for you to do, so you'd better be ready.

GET YOURSELF READY

We moms have plenty of experience getting ready—getting ourselves ready, of course, but maybe even more so getting others ready. We have to get everyone else in the household ready for school every morning, for soccer practice on Saturday, for church on Sunday. But until Mom's ready, no one can go anywhere. As a mom, you must get yourself ready first before getting your kids ready. If you try to get the kids ready first, you will never have time to get yourself ready. And again, if Momma's not ready, nobody's going anywhere.

As much as we would like to help others get ready—as much as we'd like to get our loved ones "ready" for what God has for them—the truth is, everyone must prepare himself for doing the work of the kingdom. If you spend all your time trying to get your spouse ready to fulfill God's call on his or her life, you yourself will never be ready to answer God's call on your own life. You must get yourself ready. Don't spend all your focus readying someone else. Focus on Jesus as you work on getting yourself ready to fulfill His call on your life.

STEPS TO GETTING READY

SET HEALTHY BOUNDARIES

One key to remaining focused on getting yourself ready is to establish firm boundaries. Allow the Lord to build strong, healthy boundaries in your life so you can stay focused on your relationship with Him and the work He has called you to do.

Sometimes, the most compelling inspiration for those we might be trying to help get ready is for them to see us running hard after God. We can't shake it into them, we can't beat it into them, and we can't even preach it into them if they don't want to receive it. But when we live it out for them to see, the Holy Spirit can use our lives, and His power that's released through our prayer times, to prompt a total turnaround in the lives of others. Yes, God is the God of the total turnaround.

SIT AT THE FEET OF JESUS

Getting ready means coming to the place where you are supposed to be. When you are running hard after God and His purposes for your life, you have to sit more than ever. Sounds paradoxical, doesn't it? Yet running and sitting go together.

What do I mean? The harder we are running after God and His will for our lives, the more we need to sit at His feet in prayer. Sometimes, when we are running hard, we rush right past the place of sitting. And that's how we end up tripping and falling. In order to get ourselves ready, we must sit at God's feet daily. As we spend time in His presence, we hear His marching orders, allow Him to deal with our hearts and attitudes, and respond to His *"still small voice"* (1 Kings 19:12 KJV).

We see the importance of sitting at Jesus's feet in the following passage from Luke's gospel:

> *As Jesus and his disciples were on their way, he came to a village where a woman named Martha opened her home to him. She had a sister called Mary, who sat at the Lord's feet listening to what he said. But Martha was distracted by all the preparations that had to be made. She came to him and asked, "Lord, don't you care that my sister has left me to do the work by myself? Tell her to help me!"*
>
> *"Martha, Martha," the Lord answered, "you are worried and upset about many things, but few things are needed—or indeed only one. Mary has chosen what is better, and it will not be taken away from her."* (Luke 10:38–42)

Sometimes, we get caught up in the idea of taking action—and not the kind of action God has in mind. Jesus told Martha that Mary's kind of action—sitting at His feet—was the most important kind. It seems that our natural tendency is to be out of balance. We either have too much action or we don't have enough. Or we have too much of the wrong type of action.

Martha had plenty of "action" going on, but it wasn't the right kind. Sitting at the Lord's feet in prayer is the most important action. Listening to the Lord's voice as we abide in His presence is the most important action. We should do this type of "action" daily. For it's at His feet that we receive our marching orders for the rest of our day, our week, and, ultimately, our entire lives.

TAKE ACTION

Once we've sat at the feet of Jesus long enough to know His will for us, we are ready to take action. The Word of God tells us *"faith without works is dead"* (James 2:20 KJV). In other words, having faith is good as long as we have the action that goes along with it. *"Faith comes by hearing, and hearing by the word of God"* (Romans 10:17 NKJV). When God speaks to us with a revelatory word, faith rises up within us. It's up to us to respond in faith by taking the necessary action.

Sometimes—probably most of the time, in fact—the action God demands will take us far outside our comfort zones. But I have learned that if we don't leave our comfort zones, we will never penetrate or enter into our potential zones.

BE IN THE RIGHT PLACE AT THE RIGHT TIME

We see faith in action vividly portrayed in the life of Esther, someone who dedicated herself to getting ready. When she went to the palace to compete for the hand of King Xerxes, with the ulterior motive of saving her people, the Jews, from destruction, no one was permitted to go with her. She had to go alone, after deciding for herself to accept the weighty risks involved. She didn't understand everything; she didn't have a contract guaranteeing her safety or success when she left her comfort zone, the home where she had been raised by her cousin Mordecai. She had to take the required action, by faith, in order to position herself correctly for the ultimate preservation of her people.

Mordecai had a cousin named Hadassah, whom he had brought up because she had neither father nor mother. This young woman, who was also known as Esther, had a lovely figure and was beautiful. Mordecai had taken her as his own daughter when her father and mother died. When the king's order and edict had been proclaimed, many young women were brought to the citadel of Susa and put under the care of Hegai. Esther also was taken to the king's palace and entrusted to Hegai, who had charge of the harem.

(Esther 2:7–8)

King Xerxes put out a search for beautiful young virgins. (See Esther 2:4.) And Esther qualified. I'm sure her candidacy for queen came as a huge surprise for Esther, an orphan who had been through her share of grief and despair from the loss of both her parents. I imagine this new window of opportunity was quite intimidating for her. Just think about it: someone you have never met gathers you up with a bunch of other girls you don't know and takes you all to a place where you have never been. I like adventure, but all that would have even been too much for me as a young woman. Yet I believe there was something inside Esther that told her she was supposed to take a huge step of faith. And that "something" was the prompting of the Holy Spirit.

Guided by the Holy Spirit, Esther proceeded to the palace. By force of character, she caught the eye of Hegai, who was in charge of the harem.

She pleased him and won his favor. Immediately he provided her with her beauty treatments and special food. He assigned to her seven female attendants selected from the king's palace and moved her and her attendants into the best place in the harem.

(Esther 2:9)

Esther went for it, all right. She took the required action to get herself ready for her royal destiny. And because her action took her to the right place, at the right time, and among the right people, she immediately experienced favor in the midst of her circumstances.

When we get ourselves to the place where we are supposed to be, God puts us in the best position possible. When we are in the right place, at the right time, and get ourselves ready, we receive God's best. We set ourselves up for the Lord's blessings. Just get where you are supposed to go and be who you are supposed to be.

SUBMIT TO THE "BEAUTY TREATMENTS"

Before a young woman's turn came to go in to King Xerxes, she had to complete twelve months of beauty treatments prescribed for the women, six months with oil of myrrh and six with perfumes and cosmetics. (Esther 2:12)

Esther wasn't ready until she had completed her regimen of beauty treatments. Yes, Esther positioned herself in the right place by taking the required action, then she took the next step of getting herself ready by submitting to the prescribed beauty treatments.

Part of getting ourselves ready to fulfill God's purposes is submitting to and receiving our "beauty treatments" in the Spirit. As we sit at the Lord's feet daily, we are saturated in the oil of His presence. In the presence of the Lord, we are changed. Our hearts, our attitudes, and even our very countenances transform as we sit in the glorious presence of the Lord.

I believe in doing all we can do with what we are given to work with on the outside. I thank the Lord for makeup—foundation, eyeliner, blush, and mascara. But it's the inside that causes the outside to glow with the glorious presence of the Lord. True beauty really does come from the inside out. When the Lord heals us of bitterness, hurt, and other negative emotions and scars, our outward appearance will reflect the inner newness we feel.

We humans are triune beings: we are spirits, we have a soul, and we inhabit a natural body. Since we really are spirit beings, our spiritual state causes even our natural, external appearance to change. I always say, "Sin makes us ugly, but the presence of the Lord makes us beautiful."

SURROUND YOURSELF WITH THE RIGHT PEOPLE

When the turn came for Esther (the young woman Mordecai had adopted, the daughter of his uncle Abihail) to go to the king, she asked for nothing other than what Hegai, the king's eunuch who was in charge of the harem, suggested. And Esther won the favor of everyone who saw her. (Esther 2:15)

Not only do we have to be in the right place at the right time, but we must be in the presence of the right people. Esther succeeded in her quest not only because she was in the right place at the right time, but also because she was among the right people.

When we position ourselves in the right place, at the right time, with the right people, all we have to do is be seen. Favor is just waiting for us to be seen in the right place at the right time with the right people. Esther met all three of these conditions and she blew the competition away. Even so, she acted with humility; she wasn't out to "get all she could." She wasn't focused on herself. She simply wanted whatever it was that Hegai said the king would desire for her. As we listen to what the Holy Spirit says our heavenly Father wants for us, we will succeed and proceed to the next season. When the favor of God is upon our lives, we can't help but be successful.

There were some "wrong people" in the palace when Esther arrived, but the king was not aware of it until the righteous lifestyle of Esther and her cousin Mordecai exposed those people who had manipulated their way into the king's palace.

We read of two such individuals in the following passage:

During the time Mordecai was sitting at the king's gate, Bigthana and Teresh, two of the king's officers who guarded the doorway, became angry and conspired to assassinate King Xerxes. But Mordecai found out about the plot and told Queen Esther, who in turn reported it to the king, giving credit to Mordecai.
(Esther 2:21–22)

Just as God exposed the ill-intentioned people to the king, He wants to expose "wrong people" in our lives, too—those who would harm us or derail us from fulfilling our God-given purpose. Once He has done so, we need to distance ourselves from those who stand opposed to the Lord's purposes and instead surround ourselves with the right people. One major way we prepare ourselves for the next level is by having the right people around us—faithful followers of the Lord Jesus Christ who have our best interests at heart and prize the ways of God above the ways of man.

FIND FAVOR WITH GOD

Now the King was attracted to Esther more than to any of the other women, and she won his favor and approval more than any of the other virgins. So he set a royal crown on her head and made her queen instead of Vashti. (Esther 2:17)

We can't run and hide. We have to be seen in order for the favor of the Lord to be extended to us. When the Father sees we are faithfully committed to getting to where we are supposed to be, having the heart we are supposed to have, and responding in obedience when the King calls upon us, even when it seems inconvenient, His favor will be all over us, propelling us to the next level. And when we have the favor of God, we can't help but have the favor of man. God has favor waiting for us; all we have to do is show up—in the right place, at the right time, with the right people.

The favor of God never ceases to amaze me. My ministry, an overtly Christian organization, has received generous checks in the mail from pro-fessed atheists. We receive donations from business people who aren't believ-ers. When the favor of God is upon us, we can't help but have the favor of man.

> GOD HAS FAVOR WAITING FOR US; ALL WE HAVE TO DO IS SHOW UP.

Recently, I received a letter with a $5,000 check enclosed. The letter read, "Although I'm an atheist and I don't believe in God, I appreciate all the work you do for the community, so I'm enclosing a $5,000 check." I shouted with joy, "Well, You go ahead, God!" The donor went on to explain that he saw the fruit of what my ministry was doing and that was his reason for supporting us. He said, in essence, "Government-sponsored programs don't work, yet I'm forced to support them with my tax dollars. But I have seen and heard about the results of Joy Ministries, so I want to give back to an organization that's truly making a difference in the community."

When you have nonbelievers sending you money for your Christian ministry, that's nothing but the favor of God. This type of miracle has happened over and over again in my ministry. Why? Because we're doing what God has told us to do, in the place He has told us to do it. As we are in the right place, at the right time, doing the right thing, God puts His favor on all our efforts.

The psalmist prayed, *"May the favor of the Lord our God rest on us; establish the work of our hands for us—yes, establish the work of our hands"* (Psalm 90:17). God establishes the work of our hands for us when we have His favor resting upon us. The king was attracted to Esther's obedience and the King of Kings is attracted to *our* obedience. Yes, obedience attracts the favor of the King.

God's stamp of approval will get you everywhere you need to go. You simply get yourself ready. Esther had to focus on herself. She had to go to the palace by herself. She couldn't worry about everyone else. If she did, she would have missed her destiny in the Lord.

LIVE RIGHTEOUSLY

When the report about the assassination plot of Bigthana and Teresh against King Xerxes *"was investigated and found to be true, the two officials were hanged on a gallows. All this was recorded in the book of the annals in the presence of the king"* (Esther 2:23).

Mordecai's act of righteousness was recorded in the king's book. It was recorded, but not yet rewarded. You may have done righteous things year after year, day after day, during your season of "get ready." Those acts of righteousness—whether done on the job, for your family, in your other relationships, or elsewhere—were recorded by the Lord at the time you performed them. They were immediately recorded, but it's possible they have yet to be rewarded.

Good news—reward day is approaching! God tests us to make sure we aren't in it for the reward. And once we have passed the time test, God rewards what He has previously recorded. So, if you've been waiting, get ready for your rewards in the form of promotion and crossover.

GET READY FOR THE CROSSOVER

Whenever it's time to cross over to a new level, God always supernaturally parts the waters so we may reach the other side, as He did for Moses and the children of Israel during the Exodus from Egypt. Our God is bigger than any body of water; He is stronger than any obstacle or challenge that would try to prevent us from crossing over into our season of blessing.

Stay encouraged. You are about to cross over to the place of limitless thinking and limitless living, if you'll submit to the process of getting ready.

2

COMMANDED TO TAKE THE LAND

If God commands us to do or not do something, we need to take Him seriously. When God gave Moses the Ten Commandments, He intended for them to be just that—commandments. They weren't the "ten suggestions."

Sometimes, God commands us to "take the land"—to seize a particular dream, overcome a particular enemy, or push a particular limitation out of the way. At other times, He may command us not to do something because it saddens Him or fails to edify us and others.

We must always keep in mind that the commands God gives us are motivated by His unconditional, unfailing love for us. God's commands are never given out of anger, hatred, or a desire to rule us with a heavy hand. Rather, His commands are always designed in love, to protect and guide us along the path that leads us to His very best for our lives.

GOD'S COMMANDS REFLECT HIS LOVE

God's love for us is always unconditional and forever unfailing. It is constant, everlasting, and sure. Other people may truly love us, but their love can fail us or let us down. God's love isn't like that. It never falls short of what we need or want. God's love for us is inexhaustible and reliable.

Have you ever been in a relationship with someone who looked to you to meet all his or her emotional needs? Such relationships are exhausting. No human being, no matter how wonderful, can meet all of the emotional needs of another. Only God can do that. Maybe today, you are expecting another person to meet all your emotional needs. That's a sure way to destroy a relationship—sucking the life out of another person by demanding that he or she satisfy needs that can be met only by the Lord and His unfailing love.

Again, when we hear God's commands, we must keep in mind that each of them is motivated by God's heart of unconditional, unfailing love for us. A young child who hears his parent say, "I'm doing this for your own good because I love you," doesn't usually understand. He is too focused on his immediate desire and the disappointment of not having that desire granted. But when he grows older, he gets it, especially when he has children of his own.

LOVE THAT DESIRES FRUITFULNESS

As spiritual "children" who are not mature in the things of God, we are apt to be blinded to the fact that the Lord is working to produce fruit in our lives. God's heart of love for us may command us in a certain direction or "plant" us in a certain place or situation that is not always appealing to our flesh.

Jesus said, *"Very truly I tell you, unless a kernel of wheat falls to the ground and dies, it remains only a single seed. But if it dies, it produces many* seeds" (John 12:24). When we are planted in the right place, we will never fail to bear fruit. When we are successfully planted, the seeds fall to the ground and die. When we sense the dying process occurring, our inclination is to get out of there. Our flesh wants to run. But the longer we stay planted, the larger our root system will grow. The deeper the roots, the greater the fruits. What are we running from? It may be just the thing we need to take us to the next level.

We need to get out of God's way and stand in His will. Too often, we get out of His will and stand in His way. God's best is always worth whatever price we must pay for obediently following His commands. Remember, those commands or instructions are motivated by God's heart of unfailing, unconditional love for us.

LOVE THAT DESIRES RIGHT LIVING

One way God leads us is by the commands He has given us, which are intended to guide our steps in the right direction. Psalm 107, like many passages in the Bible, is an exhortation to praise the Lord for His unfailing love in that He hears the prayers of those in need and saves them. Part of it reads:

> Then they cried out to the Lord in their trouble, and he delivered them from their distress. **He led them by a straight way** to a city where they could settle. Let them give thanks to the Lord for **his unfailing love** and his wonderful deeds for mankind, for he satisfies the thirsty and fills the hungry with good things. (Psalm 107:6–9)

God's unfailing love saves us from sin and distress. God's unfailing love rescues, heals, and delivers us. So, let us give thanks to Him daily. Let's give thanks for His unfailing love and stop complaining that we don't want to do what He's commanded us to do. It's not about us; it's about Him leading us into His best for us.

LOVE THAT NEVER LETS US DOWN

Later on, the psalmist says:

*Then they cried to the Lord in their trouble, and he **saved** them from their distress. He sent out his word and **healed** them; he **rescued** them from the grave. Let them give thanks to the Lord for his unfailing love and his wonderful deeds for mankind.* (Psalm 107:19–21)

Even when we fail God, He keeps on loving us. Thus, when others fail us, we must keep on loving them. Sometimes, God's unfailing love is reflected to us through others; other times, we need God's unfailing love because it hasn't been reflected to us by others. Either way, we should strive to be a reflection of God's unfailing love in our relationships, no matter what others may do or reflect to us.

It isn't easy to turn the other cheek and return bitterness with love. But when God is our everything, it definitely helps. The psalmist made this plea to the Lord: *"Satisfy us in the morning with your unfailing love, that we may sing for joy and be glad all our days"* (Psalm 90:14).

The revelation of God's unfailing love should cause us to sing and be filled with His joy every day, at all times, through all circumstances. When we are satisfied by God's unfailing love, then in every circumstance, we can say, "God's got this!" We can go ahead and get our praise on. We can shout, dance, and rejoice, for God is still on the throne. We must stop acting as if He's fallen off it. He's still on the throne and Jesus is at the right hand of the Father, interceding for us. (See Romans 8:34.) God's unfailing love for us means He has our back, no matter what we may face along the way. Let's give Him a shout of praise right now. Hallelujah!

> GOD'S UNFAILING LOVE FOR US MEANS HE HAS OUR BACK, NO MATTER WHAT WE MAY FACE.

SALVATION—EVIDENCE OF GOD'S LOVE

God's unfailing love is not a license to sin. Rather, it actually serves as the route out of sin through His provision of salvation.

The psalmist prayed, *"Show us your unfailing love, LORD, and grant us your salvation"* (Psalm 85:7). Salvation is the act, or the evidence, of God's unfailing love. To receive and "cash in on" God's unfailing love, we must repent of wrongdoing and then receive forgiveness. John tells us, *"If we confess our sins, he is faithful and just and will forgive us our sins and purify us from all unrighteousness"* (1 John 1:9).

According to Proverbs 28:13, *"Whoever conceals their sins does not prosper, but the one who confesses and renounces them finds mercy."* Prosper is defined as "to succeed in an enterprise or activity; to become strong and flourishing." When we confess our sins and repent of them, the unfailing, unconditional love of God causes us to thrive, succeed, and flourish.

If we don't confess our sins but attempt to cover them up, or deny that we were sinful, our blessings are cut off. We will not prosper, succeed, flourish, or thrive; rather, we will begin to dry up in all areas of life. We may experience death emotionally, spiritually, financially, mentally, and even physically. But as we embrace God's unfailing love through His plan of salvation, we can find His mercy and prosper in every area of life.

If you would like to embrace God's unfailing love and plan of salvation for your life, please pray the following:

Dear heavenly Father,

I confess that I am a sinner in need of Your mercy and grace. I acknowledge that Your Son Jesus Christ paid the price for my sins— purchasing my salvation—by dying on the cross for me and by rising again, thereby defeating the curse of sin and death. I desire to prosper and pursue Your plan for my life. Please forgive me for my sins—I repent of them. Please cleanse me and make me Your child. In Jesus's name I pray. Amen.

After we have confessed our sins, we are able to experience God's total restoration in our lives. This is true especially when we go beyond confessing our sins to the Lord by acknowledging them to our fellow believers. James 5:16 exhorts us, *"Confess your sins to each other and pray for each other so that you may be healed. The prayer of a righteous person is powerful and effective."*

If we have sinned against another person, it's often appropriate to humble ourselves and ask for that person's forgiveness, too. God blesses and gives grace to the humble. (See James 4:6.) Pray and ask the Holy Spirit if there's anyone in your life from whom you need to seek forgiveness. And then, finally, forgive yourself for all of your past mistakes and sins. Sometimes, forgiving ourselves is the hardest part.

IN LIGHT OF GOD'S UNFAILING LOVE...

OBEY HIS COMMANDS

A crucial key to prospering and achieving success is obeying the commands or instructions that God gives us in His Word.

> *Keep this Book of the Law always on your lips; meditate on it day and night, so that you may be careful to do everything written in it. Then you will be prosperous and successful.* (Joshua 1:8)

When we are careful to obey His Word and live according to its teachings and precepts, we will be blessed and highly favored. We will be the head and not the tail; we will be above and not beneath. (See Deuteronomy 28:13.) And, plainly stated, we can be prosperous and successful in everything we set our hands to do.

Jesus said to His disciples:

> *If you love me, keep my commands....Whoever has my commands and keeps them is the one who loves me. The one who loves me will be loved by my Father, and I too will love them and show myself to them.* (John 14:15, 21)

When we are in a love relationship with our heavenly Father, it becomes our heart's desire to obey His commands, which were given with our best interests in mind. For those who seek to follow His

COMMANDED TO TAKE THE LAND 41

commands and live by His standards, the rewards are beyond compare. We get to take the land—and then some.

Obedience to God's commands always results in showers of blessings. There are abundant blessings on the other side of obedience. Once we have crossed over to the side of obedience, the blessings of God chase us down and eventually overtake us.

We have to know by faith that blessings are waiting for us on the other side. When we struggle to obey Father God's commands, we must focus on what we know by faith—that abundant blessings await us. If we just suck it up for a little while, we will step into the overflow of blessings that's waiting just across the bridge of obedience.

Proverbs 13:13 says, *"Whoever scorns instruction will pay for it, but whoever respects a command is rewarded."* Yes, rewards are waiting for us! I've learned that every time God asks me to do something I don't want to do—I mean, something I *really, really* don't want to do—that's the very thing that will launch me into the place of abundant blessings in every area. This has happened to me time and time again. I can't say that it's made it any easier for me to walk in obedience to the commands or instructions God gives me, but I can say that the Lord has a perfect track record. When I look back at the track record, I can take a step of faith and act in obedience, knowing that God's best awaits me.

"If you love me, keep my commands," Jesus said. When the love of God is our motivation, it makes obedience easier. We obey the Father's commands and directions to take the land because we are motivated by our heart's love for Him. Please notice that I said "easier," not *easy.* We don't need "easy." We just need "possible" and with God, all things are possible. (See Matthew 19:26; Mark 10:27.) God will always give us the grace to stand in the place of obedience.

SUBMIT TO THE AUTHORITIES INSTITUTED BY GOD

It had been over twenty-five years since my first speeding ticket when I went and ruined my great record again. When I was handed the second speeding ticket of my life, I had been going forty-eight miles per hour in a thirty-five-mph zone. About one week prior, I had noticed a squad car was often parked by the roundabout that I drive through multiple times a week. I thought the cop was looking for people breaking a traffic law in the roundabout. But I can remember wondering to myself what the speed limit was. I checked my GPS, which usually registers that type of information, but it was blank. I tried to look for a sign, but never found one.

Then, one week later, I was taking my daughter, Destiny, to dance class and we were running behind. It was the worst day of my entire year. I was upset with her for not being ready on time, I was disgusted with the events of the day, and I had the pedal to the metal.

When the young police officer pulled me over, my first thought was, *It wasn't my fault!* Sound familiar? Our flesh always wants to make excuses. I was shocked because I honestly hadn't realized I was breaking the law. But I somehow managed to remain calm, cool, and collected—at least temporarily. When the officer told me how fast I had been driving, I responded, "Could I please have grace this time, Officer?"

Let's just say he didn't feel led to extend grace to me that day. When he refused my request, it was all I could do to bite my tongue. The power of the Holy Spirit supernaturally enabled me to keep my mouth shut. In the body of Christ, I tend to be a "mouth," but I managed to bite my tongue, smiled a weird-looking smile, and said nothing more. Trust me, that was a miracle. I wanted to tell him there would come a time when he would need God's grace. I wanted to tell him I knew God had extended grace to him many times already; how could he possibly refuse to extend grace to me just this once? But I didn't say any of that—thank the Lord!

After the officer handed me the ticket, Destiny started laughing at the look on my face as I continued to hold back my words. She then took a picture of me with her cell phone and posted all the details on Facebook. I was steaming mad at this point. After all, she was the one who caused me to speed. She was the one running late.

Needless to say, it was a long night. After dropping Destiny off at the dance studio, I went and got some chocolate to ease my pain. It was then that I heard the voice of the Lord say, "Don't ever think you are above the laws of the land." I got it! I delight to submit to the law of the Lord—and the land. And when I don't, I just fake it till I make it.

The apostle Paul gave the following instructions on the "laws of the land" in his letter to the Romans:

> *Let everyone be subject to the governing authorities, for there is no authority except that which God has established. The authorities that exist have been established by God. Consequently, whoever rebels against the authority is rebelling against what God has instituted, and those who do so will bring judgment on themselves.*
>
> (Romans 13:1–2)

All authority has been established by our loving God. Those who rebel against the authorities that God has established are actually rebelling against God Himself. Let's not bring judgment on ourselves by rebelling against that which God has instituted. That would not be wise. Plus, the Word says, *"Rebellion is as the sin of witchcraft, and stubbornness is as iniquity and idolatry"* (1 Samuel 15:23 KJV). We must not dally with spiritual witchcraft by speaking against those in authority, especially those in spiritual authority. God says in His Word, *"Touch not mine anointed"* (1 Chronicles 16:22 KJV; Psalm 105:15 KJV). Let's not "touch" them with our negative words. We don't excuse sin in the lives of our leaders, but speaking against them in a rebellious way reveals sin in our hearts—sin that will hinder us from taking the land that God has for us.

Sometimes, people who have been abused by an authority figure develop a mind-set of rebellion against anyone in authority. But just because someone in the past misused or abused his authority, it doesn't mean we can overlook God's principle of authority. One of our greatest keys to stepping into everything that God has for us and taking all the land our Father intends for us to inherit is understanding authority, respecting authority, and submitting to those in authority over us, in the various areas of our lives.

Even the respect of spiritual authority is lacking in the lives of many believers today. Authority is for our protection; God designed and established it with our best interests in mind. When we are under authority, we are under an umbrella of protection that God has provided for our own well-being.

The letter to the Hebrews expresses a similar sentiment:

> *Have confidence in your leaders and submit to their authority, because they keep watch over you as those who must give an account. Do this so that their work will be a joy, not a burden, for that would be of no benefit to you.* (Hebrews 13:17)

We remain under the protection of God's authority when we obey His commands. On the job, in school, in churches and other organizations, and within our communities, we are faced with authority figures we must respect, obey, and submit to. If our ultimate authority is God, we more readily obey the other authorities He has established. When a person enters a prison, a detention home, or a mental hospital, one of the first things he must learn is to obey and submit to authority. In many cases, one contributing factor to his being placed in such an institution was a lack of respect and submission to authority.

Even if someone in authority over us has mistreated us, we can't throw out the baby with the bathwater, so to speak. God's Word is always God's Word. As we submit in healthy ways to God-ordained authority figures, we can experience God's blessings and protection on our way to taking all the land He has commanded us to take.

GOD COMMANDS HIS ANGELS CONCERNING YOU

> *If you say, "The Lord is my refuge," and you make the Most High your dwelling, no harm will overtake you, no disaster will come near your tent. For he will command his angels concerning you to guard*

you in all your ways; they will lift you up in their hands, so that you
will not strike your foot against a stone.   (Psalm 91:9–12)

When we live under God's protective hand by submitting to His authority and following His law, He even commands His angels concerning us. God's will is for us to not merely see the land we are supposed to possess but to take possession of it. Seeing the land is one thing; taking possession of it is entirely different. Yes, we have to see the land before we possess it, but seeing the land doesn't guarantee that we will possess it. When we have angelic forces working on our behalf, possessing the land becomes far more feasible.

Possess is another way of saying "to take ownership of." God wants us to take ownership of all the land He has reserved for us. He wants us to fulfill our life's purpose in its entirety. *Possession* also implies the acts of obtaining and maintaining. God wants us to obtain and maintain His peace, His joy, His presence, His love, His divine health, His abundant financial blessings, and more. What we possess, we own, no matter the time, no matter the season, no matter what's happening around us, to us, or through us. When we possess the land, we own it. With the help of God's angels, the land is ours when we walk in obedience to God's commands.

3

THINK BIG

Limits are not always a bad thing. There are many areas where we would do well to set more, or stricter, limits than we do right now. For example, it is wise to limit the quantity of food we eat, the hours of television we watch, and the amount of time we spend on our electronic devices. It's advantageous to limit the words we speak, the conversations we engage in, and our exposure to certain television shows or types of music. Limitations are important in training children; we set boundaries, both physical and moral, for their safety and well-being.

But there are plenty of areas in our lives where God wants us to experience no limits whatsoever. Our God-given potential, our zeal for advancing the kingdom, our divine dreams—these areas should be without limit. And when limits exist on these areas—whether those limits are put there by other people and institutions or whether we ourselves are responsible for them—it hinders God's operation in and through us.

GOD'S LOVE IS UNCONDITIONAL AND WITHOUT LIMIT.

Let's talk about the love of God for a moment. His love for us is limitless! Other people, no matter how much they may love us, have limits on their love. They may reduce or retract their affections. Not so God. His love is unconditional and without limit. It's hard to comprehend His limitless love for us—so hard, in fact, that we may doubt its existence.

Have you set limits on God's love for you? Have you set limits on what you "think" God can do in you, through you, and for you? Sometimes, we are capable of limitless thinking on behalf of other people, yet not for ourselves. If that's the case for you, God wants to totally turn that around for you today. He wants to establish within you a mind-set of limitless thinking that will last a lifetime.

All of the people in the Bible who thought big saw "big" come to pass. All who asked big of God received big from Him. All who expected big were satisfied. All who thought big, asked big, and expected big were blown away by all of the amazing things they saw God do in response.

Today, the same can be true for you. There's no limit to what God wants to do in you, through you, and for you. It all begins with your allowing the Lord to help you to think big.

ACKNOWLEDGE HOW BIG GOD IS

Thinking big is the first step to actually seeing "big" manifested. You think big by acknowledging who God is, by remembering all that He has done for you personally, and by meditating on His Word, which proclaims the eternal truth about His nature and character.

Then always stay focused on these truths: what God has done before, He will do again, because He is *"the same yesterday and today and forever"* (Hebrews 13:8). And He is no respecter of persons—in other words, He shows no favoritism. (See Acts 10:34.) What He has done for others, He will do for you.

The first key to thinking big is simply acknowledging who God is. In case you have never really thought about it, God is a big, **BIG** God. We get so caught up in our little lives and limited mind-sets that we don't even realize it when we've put God in a box, so to speak. God is BIG— without limits! And we need to think like God thinks—big!

When we recognize and acknowledge how big God is, we can begin to think like He does. We're quick to acknowledge and complain about the size of our problems and tricky situations, yet we often fail to acknowledge, in the midst of a storm or battle, how big our God is.

It all starts with our mind-set. We shouldn't set our minds on the battle; we should set our minds on the truth. The truth is, God is on our side and He's got this. He's got our back, so let's go ahead and think big.

I dare you to step out of your comfort zone, think big by acknowledging God in the midst of your circumstances, and enter into your potential zone. Your potential zone is as big as your thinking allows it to be, so remove all the limits.

ACT, DON'T REACT

In the twentieth chapter of 2 Chronicles, several men went to King Jehoshaphat to warn him that a vast army was advancing speedily against him and his people.

It's one thing to know a storm or a battle is coming, but quite another when it's the size of Texas. The enemy can deceive us into thinking he's really big, yet he's nothing compared to our big God. If the enemy can trick us into thinking he's too big for us to defeat, he can blind us to the truth that our God is much, much bigger than he is.

ACT OUT OF YOUR SPIRIT

The Word tells us that Jehoshaphat was alarmed, yet he did not react out of his flesh; he acted out of his spirit. When we react out of our flesh, we think small; we freak out and fear the worst. We cry, we scream, we yell, and we produce every other manner of unproductive response. Some people even run away from God at the very time when they most need to run *to* Him, all because they aren't thinking straight.

But Jehoshaphat didn't react out of his flesh; he acted out of his spirit. He was thinking BIG!

> *Alarmed, Jehoshaphat resolved to inquire of the* LORD, *and he proclaimed a fast for all Judah. The people of Judah came together to seek help from the* LORD; *indeed, they came from every town in Judah to seek him.* (2 Chronicles 20:3–4)

In the midst of the biggest battle of Jehoshaphat's life, he inquired of the Lord because he was thinking correctly. He didn't inquire of his friends, his pastor, or his spouse. He came before the Lord in fasting and prayer and he encouraged his people to do the same.

Jehoshaphat was alarmed when he learned a vast army was coming to make war with him, but he didn't panic. When we are thinking small, we panic easily. Jehoshaphat did not react; he acted. As a result of his thinking big, he saw God do big things on his behalf. Jehoshaphat had the proper mind-set. He didn't react with his flesh, his emotions, or his natural mind.

Reacting to the battle we are up against only serves to acknowledge how big and powerful our enemy is. But when we act out of our spirit, we acknowledge how big and powerful God is and we declare our unfailing trust that He will bring us through.

ACT BASED ON WHAT GOD TELLS YOU

Jehoshaphat proclaimed a fast for the nation so he might hear from God on how to handle the situation. He was thinking, *My big God has got this; I simply need to hear from Him regarding what He wants me to do.*

Not only did Jehoshaphat seek the Lord, but he proclaimed a fast for all Judah. Everyone in the surrounding towns came together to fast and seek God's direction. The people responded to Jehoshaphat's leadership, following his example. If Jehoshaphat had panicked and come unglued, most likely, the people around him would have done the same thing. They would have made an emotional response, thereby giving the enemy a good chance of defeating them.

Emotional responses open the door to the enemy, but when we act out of our spirit, looking to the Lord for how to handle the situations we face, we will come out on the winning side, claiming victory as ours.

Jehoshaphat *"resolved to inquire of the LORD"*—not his best friend, not his experienced fighting men, not his family, but the Lord. When we inquire of the Lord, we get His opinion and gain insights into His "big thinking" on the matter at hand.

ACT WITH CONFIDENCE IN YOUR GREAT BIG GOD

When the people gathered at the temple, Jehoshaphat stood before them and prayed. He began by acknowledging God as the all-powerful, all-knowing God. He prayed, *"Power and might are in your hand, and no one can withstand you"* (2 Chronicles 20:6).

When we acknowledge God for who He is, we don't have any trouble giving Him control of every situation. But when we fail to recognize who God is, we start acting out of our own strength, operating as if we're the ones in control. Trust me, we don't want our little, limited mind-sets to be in charge of drawing up the battle plan when we are at war. It's at those times, more than ever, that we need to think big, like God thinks.

Jehoshaphat acknowledged who God was in his situation. As a result, he looked to God for the solution to the problem. We need to recognize and acknowledge who God is in the midst of our trying circumstances. Sometimes, we get so caught up in acknowledging how big our opponent is, we forget that God is bigger and is in control.

This is exactly what happened to most of the spies Moses sent to scope out the Promised Land. Except for Joshua and Caleb, they quaked in their boots over the size of the people there, likening themselves to grasshoppers in comparison. (See Numbers 13:32–33.)

When we panic, we attempt to do in the flesh what can be done only in the Spirit. Let me tell you, if a vast army was coming against you and you failed to recognize God and His abilities, you would lose your peace, your joy, and, ultimately, your battle.

When we get caught up in the flesh, we try to do things ourselves; we claim every battle as our own. But when we remember who God is, in the midst of our circumstances, we can let Him have control. We can trust Him with the outcome because the battle belongs to the Lord. (See 1 Samuel 17:47.)

REMEMBER GOD'S FAITHFULNESS

As Jehoshaphat continued his prayer aloud, he reminded the people about everything God had already done for them. He said, *"Our God, did you not drive out the inhabitants of this land before your people Israel and give it forever to the descendants of Abraham your friend?"* (2 Chronicles 20:7). When we recall everything the Lord has done for us in the past, it builds our faith and boosts our ability to "think big" for both the present moment and the future. We must think like the Lord thinks and let Him take control in order to emerge victorious from our current situation.

As we express gratitude to God for bringing us through difficult trials in the past, we encourage ourselves in the Lord. When it comes down to it, God has never let us down. And He's never going to fail us. We just need to encourage ourselves by remembering God's faithfulness in the past and stand on the promises of God for today.

ACT, THEN WATCH AS GOD RESPONDS

King Jehoshaphat continued with his prayer, saying:

If calamity comes upon us, whether the sword of judgment, or plague or famine, we will stand in your presence before this temple that

bears your Name and will cry out to you in our distress, and you will
hear us and save us.   (2 Chronicles 20:9)

Jehoshaphat stated his firm belief that no matter what happened, God would respond. If calamity does indeed come upon us, all we have to do is cry out to God. God always hears us and He is faithful to deliver us, no matter how big the battle.

Jehoshaphat demonstrated his total dependence on the Lord when he went on to pray:

Our God, will you not judge them? For we have no power to face this
vast army that is attacking us. We do not know what to do, but our
eyes are on you.   (2 Chronicles 20:12)

When we face the reality of our inabilities—and acknowledge God's limitless, all-surpassing abilities and power—it's an awesome thing. Finding ourselves in a situation where we are desperate for God is a good place to be. We seldom receive a miracle unless we're desperate for one. God wants us to be totally dependent upon Him.

Jehoshaphat said, *"We do not know what to do..."* In other words, without God, our goose is cooked—we will be destroyed! *"We do not know what to do, **but our eyes are on you.**"* Like Jehoshaphat, we need to keep our eyes on the Lord. When we realize we can't, when we realize God can, and when we keep our eyes on God rather than on the army coming against us, we can set the stage for our miracle, all because we are thinking like God—thinking big!

We need to let God be God. He is in control, so we can stop trying to be. *"Cast your cares on the Lord and he will sustain you; he will never let the righteous be shaken"* (Psalm 55:22). Accept your total dependence upon Him, begin to think big like He does, and let God fight your battles all the way to victory.

GOD IS IN CONTROL, SO WE CAN STOP TRYING TO BE.

God was faithful to hear and answer Jehoshaphat's prayer. God always answers our prayers, even if He doesn't always answer when or how we want Him to. He doesn't always answer the way we think He "should." But He always hears our prayers and answers them. His answer may be "no." It may be "not now." His answer may be "wait a while." But He always answers.

FACE THE ENEMY HEAD-ON WITH FAITH

Later on, we read about God sending Jahaziel, one of His servants, to speak the word of the Lord to Jehoshaphat:

> *This is what the* LORD *says to you: "Do not be afraid or discouraged because of this vast army. For the battle is not yours, but God's."*
>
> (2 Chronicles 20:15)

When we keep our gaze on the army that is coming against us, we can easily become fearful and begin to "think small" when we compare them with the size of our own army. Small thinking leads to discouragement, which tempts us to throw in the towel and stop trying altogether. But God tells us not to be afraid or discouraged because the battle is not ours; the battle belongs to the Lord and He never wants us to give up or give in.

Fear can be paralyzing. We shouldn't allow ourselves to dwell in fear. The opposite of fear is faith. When we walk in faith, we remain confident that God will come through for us. We know God will take care of the enemy. When we think big, quitting is never an option.

Still speaking through Jahaziel, God told Jehoshaphat, "*Tomorrow, march out against them*" (2 Chronicles 20:16 NLT). In other words, He was saying, "Face the enemy immediately. Do it first thing in the morning. Don't put it off."

We shouldn't delay when facing our enemies or dealing with the storms that come our way. We must meet them head-on at the first chance we get. If we put off confronting our opponents and adversaries, we give them an opportunity to mess with our minds and "shrink our thinking," so to speak. But if we are thinking big, we respond immediately and don't delay dealing with stuff. Why? Because we expect big victory and we can't imagine any other outcome.

Putting off facing the enemy only magnifies our fears and intimidation. Running away only keeps us in fear and bondage. But we can rob difficult circumstances and actual adversaries of their power by confronting them and not cowering fearfully in the corner. Intimidation is a universal battle tactic. If our enemy can get us to think he is able to blow us off the map in no time, our defeat is almost guaranteed. Don't be intimidated. Face the enemy head-on, at the first opportunity. Then, the enemy will be the one who's running scared. Tomorrow, go out and face your enemies with your big thinking and your big God!

TRUST GOD TO EXPOSE THE ENEMY'S SCHEMES

God spoke through Jahaziel to reveal the plans of the enemy to King Jehoshaphat ahead of time. (See 2 Chronicles 20:15–17.) Knowing the enemy's position and plan of attack gives us a major advantage.

What benefits there are to cultivating a powerful prayer life! If we live a life of prayer in which we abide in the presence of God, He may reveal the enemy's plans to us. That way, we can think big, trusting that God will tell us everything we need to know, when we need to know it. When we think big, we believe God will let us see and hear everything we need to.

The Lord told Jehoshaphat that he would not have to fight the battle. (See 2 Chronicles 20:17.) All he had to do was take his position, stand firm, and see the deliverance that the Lord would give him.

What is your position? It should be worshipping God and standing on His Word. God created you to worship Him. Worship God in big ways, in all you think, say, and do—in how you live your life. When you think big, it's easy to let go, let God be God, and get your praise on, even in the midst of the battle.

ABIDE IN GOD'S WORD

Another vital step to expand your thinking is to abide in God's Word, which spells out the truth about God's nature and character. When you know the truth, God's Word, it sets you free, as Jesus explained to His disciples. (See John 8:32.) Most of us need to be set free in order to think big.

The enemy tells all kinds of lies to try to get us to believe in his efforts and keep us bound up in limited thinking. When the enemy gets us to "buy the lie," the lie puts us in a box of small, insecure, limited thinking. When we're trapped in that box, the enemy whispers all manner of fearful thoughts in our ear, trying to keep us inside the box, lest we try to escape. The devil's lies put us in the box of small, limited thinking, and the spirit of fear keeps us subject to those lies.

Good news, friend: the truths recorded in the Bible can set you free from the enemy's lies and the resulting fears. The Word of truth can launch you forth into a life of freedom ruled by a mind-set of limitless thinking.

MEDITATE ON THE WORD DAY AND NIGHT

Remember God's promise in Joshua 1:8: "*Keep this Book of the Law always on your lips; meditate on it day and night, so that you may be careful to do everything written in it. Then you will be prosperous and successful.*"

The first thing we see in this verse is that the responsibility is ours. The ball is in our court. We choose whether the Word of God dwells in our hearts or not. When the Word remains on our lips, we speak the Word day and night. To put it another way, when others are speaking gossip, bad news, and other junk, we are declaring God's Word.

The verse also tells us to meditate on the Word "*day and night.*" We need to be thinking about the Word all the time.

So, we speak the Word, we think the Word, and, finally, we do the Word. We are instructed to "*be careful to do everything written in*" God's Word. This allows us to think big—without limits.

When we think big, we will always prosper and succeed at whatever God has ordained for us to do. Too many people are trying to prosper and succeed in their own strength, while maintaining a limited mindset. Small thinking produces small fruit, while big thinking produces big fruit. The choice is yours.

KNOW WHAT GOD'S WORD SAYS ABOUT YOU

What you think about yourself is also vital. The root of small thinking usually lies in a poor self-image. *"For as* [a person] *thinks in his heart, so is he"* (Proverbs 23:7 NKJV). The enemy tries to get us to "think small" about ourselves from the very beginning—because when we do so, we also "think small" about our God, minimizing what He can and will do in us, through us, and for us. If Satan can get us to "think small," he can cripple us into believing small and doing small.

> IF SATAN CAN GET US TO "THINK SMALL," HE CAN CRIPPLE US INTO BELIEVING SMALL AND DOING SMALL.

Once again, what we think of ourselves is a self-fulfilling prophecy. We have to see ourselves as successful and fruitful. By meditating on the Word of God, we can experience a total turnaround in our thinking, beginning with our self-image. Let God turn your thoughts around today so they can line up with His thoughts about you.

Just what does God think of you? It's hard to put into words how much He loves and values you, but the Scriptures can give you an idea:

The LORD appeared to us in the past, saying: "I have loved you with an everlasting love; I have drawn you with unfailing kindness."
(Jeremiah 31:3)

"For I know the plans I have for you," declares the LORD, "plans to prosper you and not to harm you, plans to give you hope and a future."
(Jeremiah 29:11)

For you [LORD] created my inmost being; you knit me together in my mother's womb. I praise you because I am fearfully and wonderfully made; your works are wonderful, I know that full well. My frame was not hidden from you when I was made in the secret place, when I was woven together in the depths of the earth. Your eyes saw my unformed body; all the days ordained for me were written in your book before one of them came to be. (Psalm 139:13–16)

You need to think big, the way God thinks. God has big plans for you, *"plans to prosper you and not to harm you."* Poverty is not His plan for you, so don't think with an impoverished mind-set. And His intention is not to harm you. You may have been through some horrendous experiences, but God has a big, bright, and fruitful future in store for you.

Small, limited thinking leaves you hopeless. Thinking big allows you to tap into the glorious, powerful, productive potential the Lord has given you. Don't give up hope. Quitting is not part of God's plan for your life. Rebuke all limited, small thinking, and begin to dream big. Your future is bright. God knows His plans for you and how awesome those plans are. Open your heart and mind through His Word and allow Him to reveal His plan for your life. When you find out about His plan and then begin to see it manifest, the way you think will undergo a total transformation.

4

ASK AND EXPECT BIG

The word of the Lord to you today is, "Ask big!" You have been asking the Lord for too little. God wants you to ask Him for big things, because He wants to do big things in you, through you, and for you. When I get to heaven, I don't want to hear the Lord say to me, "Why didn't you ask Me for more? Why did you always ask for so little? Why were your expectations of Me so small?"

Asking and expecting big is a vital key to seeing big fruit manifest and seeing big things come to pass before your very eyes.

The biblical character of Jabez is a good example of someone who asked big of God. As a result of his boldness in asking for blessings,

Jabez received big rewards and he saw big fruit produced through his life for the kingdom of God.

> *Jabez was more honorable than his brothers....Jabez cried out to the God of Israel, "Oh, that you would bless me and enlarge my territory! Let your hand be with me, and keep me from harm so that I will be free from pain." And God granted his request.*
> (1 Chronicles 4:9–10)

Jabez was not in competition with his brothers; he simply had a heart to maintain a standard of excellence. His brothers chose the easy road, but Jabez was willing to pay the price to be more and do more for God.

Do you desire to go further and do more, as Jabez did? Or do you want to "just make it," to barely squeeze by? Are you committed to upholding a standard of excellence in all you do?

In order to maintain high standards and be more honorable than others, we must live day by day in the presence of the Lord, cultivating a spirit of worship and being committed to prayer. It's in the presence of the Lord that the Holy Spirit convicts us of sin and keeps us on the path that pleases the Father.

It's from a place of powerful prayer that we can ask big of the Lord. When our big requests come as a result of a powerful prayer life, the Holy Spirit is in the midst of them. But when our big requests are made without a commitment to the Lord, they are fleshly, carnal, and selfish. God wants us to ask big out of a pure heart and proper motives, which also result from intimate times of prayer.

Jabez wanted to be more and do more for God, and God granted his request. God wants to do the same for you today. He wants you to request it in faith through prayer, followed by actions of obedience. He wants to give you more, but you have to request it. God wants to do and give you exceedingly, abundantly above all you could ever think, ask, or even imagine. (See Ephesians 3:20.) But you must reach for it.

Will you ask big of the Lord? Will you ask the Lord to do big things in you, through you, and for you? He's just waiting to answer that prayer for you, as He did for Jabez.

ASK AND YOU SHALL RECEIVE

Jesus had a lot to say about how to ask for things in prayer. Consider the following passage from Matthew's gospel:

Ask and it will be given to you; seek and you will find; knock and the door will be opened to you. For everyone who asks receives; the one who seeks finds; and to the one who knocks, the door will be opened. (Matthew 7:7–8)

Jesus tells us, "*Ask and it will be given to you*"—not, "Ask and *maybe* you will receive it." The Bible also says, "*Take delight in the* LORD, *and he will give you the desires of your heart*" (Psalm 37:4). What a beautiful truth that is. When we are delighting ourselves in the Lord—loving God with our whole hearts, hanging out in His glorious presence—our wills are made pliable, so He may mold, shape, and direct us to desire those things that *He* desires for us. When we delight ourselves in the Lord and saturate ourselves with His presence through prayer, our requests proceed directly from the heart of God. And when we ask according to the will of God, led by His Holy Spirit, we can be confident that we will receive what we have asked for.

God always has our best interests in mind. He will always lead us to that which is best for us, and He often does this by placing specific desires in our hearts. It stands to reason that when we've been abiding in God's presence and we lose a desire for something or someone, it's usually because the Holy Spirit is leading us away from that place, object, activity, or person.

Likewise, when we begin to desire something that we never found appealing before and that thing is godly, we can trust that it is the Lord's leading. This is one way the Holy Spirit leads us to do the will of the Father.

As we continue to delight ourselves in the Lord, He gives us the desires of our hearts, because those desires correspond with the will of the Father for our lives. It's from such a pliable heart that God wants us to ask big things of Him. At this point and place, our asking big proceeds straight from the heart of God. And God's heart is always to do big things in us, through us, and for us.

When we make our big requests of the Lord, faith is key. Each of us has been given a *"measure of faith"* (Romans 12:3 KJV) and some only have faith the size of a mustard seed. Good news—that's all we need. (See Matthew 17:20; Luke 17:6.) Our measure of faith may be teeny-tiny, but that's not what counts. The key is allowing the Holy Spirit to work with our measure of faith, no matter how small it may be. It has the potential to grow like crazy if we entrust it to the Lord.

BIG THINGS *IN* YOU

God wants to do big things in you. For most of us, the first big thing God wants to do in us is to heal us. We live in a broken, messed-up world, so it makes sense that most of us have been through broken, messed-up situations that have made us into broken, messed-up people. But thank God for the saving, redeeming work of Jesus's blood and the power of the Holy Spirit to do big things in us.

God needs to do big things in us before He can do big things through us. I always tell people that the number one reason God sent me to get a master's degree in counseling was because I needed counseling myself. Yes, I have had the call of God on my life from my mother's womb, but I needed a lot of healing before I was ready and prepared to fulfill that call.

> GOD TURNS OUR TESTS INTO TESTIMONIES AND OUR MESSES INTO POWERFUL, LIFE-CHANGING MESSAGES.

God desires to do big things *in* us so we will be fully prepared and equipped for Him to do big things *through* us. If we try to do great things for God before He has helped us through our own issues, we won't produce as much fruit as we otherwise might—not to mention we're likely to make a big mess. And big messes can give God a bad name.

But God, out of His unconditional love for us, turns our tests into testimonies and our messes into powerful, life-changing messages that will help other people take the land in their own lives, if we will first yield and allow the Lord to do His work in us.

Sometimes, this work may take years to complete. We must be patient while God finishes His work in us. He will finish it, as Paul assures us:

[Be] *confident of this, that he who began a good work in you will carry it on to completion until the day of Christ Jesus.*

(Philippians 1:6)

In my case, God's work took many years. But God didn't put me on a shelf with a big red stamp that read "unusable." The degree to which I was healed became the degree to which God used me in that season. The truth is, you can't take anyone to a place where you yourself have not been or are not currently. You can't take anyone to a higher place than where you are yourself.

God wants to bring us to a place of total healing in spirit, soul, and body. Once we have allowed God to do big things in us, He is able to do big things *through* us.

Ask God to do big things in you today. Ask Him to take you to a place of total healing and submit to His timing. If you are like me, it will take years for God to totally heal you. One time when I became impatient with God, He said to me, "You didn't get in this condition overnight and you aren't going to get healed overnight." I thought He had a pretty good point.

The truth is, God's timing is perfect. We simply need to submit ourselves to the Lord and allow Him to do the necessary healing in our hearts, minds, and spirits. Aren't you glad that His loving-kindness and sweet presence serve as the anesthesia for every spiritual and emotional "heart surgery" we must undergo?

BIG THINGS *THROUGH* YOU

God wants us to ask Him to do big things in us, as Jabez did, so He may do big things through us for the benefit of His kingdom. When we are bold enough to ask big, God will grant our requests, as He did for Jabez.

Nehemiah was another man who asked for—and received—big things from God. He served as governor of Judah, yet he had a heart for ministering to the needs of others. He was deeply touched by the pain and troubles of his fellow man. Nehemiah's heart of compassion caused him to ask big of God on behalf of the Israelites, with abundant fruit resulting. When Nehemiah learned the wall of Jerusalem was broken down, its gates burned with fire, and the people in distress:

> I sat down and wept. For some days I mourned and fasted and prayed before the God of heaven. Then I said: "Lord, God of heaven, the great and awesome God, who keeps his covenant of love with those who love him and keep his commandments, let your ear be attentive and your eyes open to hear the prayer your servant is praying before you day and night for your servants, the people of Israel. I confess the sins we Israelites, including myself and my father's family, have committed against you. We have acted very wickedly toward you. We have not obeyed the commands, decrees and laws you gave your servant Moses. Remember the instruction you gave your servant Moses, saying, 'If you are unfaithful, I will scatter you among the nations, but if you return to me and obey my commands, then even if your exiled people are at the farthest horizon, I will gather them from there and bring them to the place I have chosen as a dwelling for my Name.' They are your servants and your people, whom you redeemed by your great strength and your mighty hand. Lord, let your ear be attentive to the prayer of

this your servant and to the prayer of your servants who delight in revering your name. Give your servant success today by granting him favor in the presence of this man [King Artaxerxes]."

(Nehemiah 1:4–11)

ASK BIG IN PRAYER

Nehemiah asked big of God in prayer. He asked God to grant him favor with the king, that he might do big things to help those in need. Nehemiah's heart was right and his motives were pure. He knew that in order to do big things for God, he needed to ask for God's favor in a big way.

So the king asked me, "Why does your face look so sad when you are not ill? This can be nothing but sadness of heart." I was very much afraid, but I said to the king, "May the king live forever! Why should my face not look sad when the city where my ancestors are buried lies in ruins, and its gates have been destroyed by fire?" The king said to me, "What is it you want?" Then I prayed to the God of heaven, and I answered the king, "If it pleases the king and if your servant has found favor in his sight, let him send me to the city in Judah where my ancestors are buried so that I can rebuild it." Then the king, with the queen sitting beside him, asked me, "How long will your journey take, and when will you get back?" It pleased the king to send me; so I set a time.

(Nehemiah 2:2–6)

When Nehemiah went before the king, he received just what he had asked for in prayer—big favor. The king even went above and beyond in granting the request. Nehemiah had more than enough favor and blessings to do what was on his heart to do for God's people.

Nehemiah requested a leave of absence from his position as cup-bearer in order to go on a mission trip to help those in need. Because Nehemiah had a heart for the people, the king was pleased to send him on his errand.

ASK BIG ON BEHALF OF OTHERS

Nehemiah had a heart to rebuild the walls the enemy had torn down. When you have a heart to help others rebuild the fallen walls of their lives, it will please the Father to send you and provide for you. Just be sure to ask and ask big.

When the enemy tears down literal or figurative walls in the lives of God's people, we must allow the Lord to do a work of rebuilding and restoration. Nehemiah was the willing vessel God used to do supernatural things, all because he did not hesitate to ask big of God so he could bless others.

Nehemiah wasn't afraid to push his luck and ask even more of the king.

> *I also said to him, "If it pleases the king, may I have letters to the governors of Trans-Euphrates, so that they will provide me safe-conduct until I arrive in Judah? And may I have a letter to Asaph, keeper of the royal park, so he will give me timber to make beams for the gates of the citadel by the temple and for the city wall and for the residence I will occupy?" And because the gracious hand of my God was upon me, the king granted my requests. So I went to the governors of Trans-Euphrates and gave them the king's letters. The king had also sent army officers and cavalry with me.* (Nehemiah 2:7–9)

When Nehemiah asked for letters of reference, once again, the king not only granted his request, he gave Nehemiah even more than he had asked for. Because the hand of God was upon Nehemiah, the king granted his requests—and then some. When you ask big, you have the favor of God. When you have the favor of God, you can't help but have the favor of man, for *"the king's heart is in the hand of the* LORD*"* (Proverbs 21:1 NKJV).

ASK BIG IN FAITH

When you ask God to do big things through you, it's important to ask in faith. As it says in James 1:6, *"When you ask, you must believe and not doubt.*" Moreover, Jesus said, *"Whatever you ask for in prayer, believe that you have received it, and it will be yours"* (Mark 11:24).

Too many people sit back and wait until they can see everything lining up in the natural. They wait until they have all of the money in the bank; they wait until they've assembled all of the people they think they will need to accomplish their vision. But part of asking big is asking with big faith. Nehemiah told the officials in Jerusalem:

> *"You see the trouble we are in: Jerusalem lies in ruins, and its gates have been burned with fire. Come, let us rebuild the wall of Jerusalem, and we will no longer be in disgrace." I also told them about the gracious hand of my God on me and what the king had said to me. They replied, "Let us start rebuilding." So they began this good work.* (Nehemiah 2:17–18)

You ask big of God and then you take a big leap of faith when He tells you it's time. You don't have to understand everything, nor do you need to "feel" it's the right time. When you sense in your spirit that it's God's will and God's time, you simply need to begin the good work that you have been asking God to do through you.

BIG THINGS *FOR* YOU

God wants to do big things in you, through you, and *for* you, too, if you will simply ask Him. God wants to bless you with big anointing, big favor, and big financial blessings. He doesn't want you to ask big for your own selfish gain, but for the benefit of His kingdom. When you have a pure heart and you ask big for the sake of kingdom purposes, you will be blessed.

> WHEN YOU HAVE A PURE HEART AND YOU ASK BIG FOR THE SAKE OF KINGDOM PURPOSES, YOU WILL BE BLESSED.

The Bible says, *"Those who give to the poor will lack nothing"* (Proverbs 28:27). I have seen this promise come to pass in my own life. As I've given big to help those who are less fortunate, God has brought me into a place of abundant blessings.

God wants to bless you in big ways, with refined character, steadfast integrity, surpassing joy, abundant grace, strong faith, and transcendent peace—a peace that *"transcends all understanding"* (Philippians 4:7).

So, don't forget to ask big for yourself, your family, and your loved ones. God is the God of more than enough, but many people ask and believe small for themselves.

Why don't more people ask big for themselves? Some are so hung up on their past and mistakes they have made that they feel unworthy of being blessed. Some people don't ask big for themselves because they can't conceive of the idea that God wants to bless them big time. More often than not, people don't ask God to do big things for them because they really don't believe that it pleases the Lord when they do so.

The truth is, God wants us to ask Him to bless us and our loved ones—big time. He delights in fulfilling this request of ours. He honored Jabez when he asked for big blessings, didn't He? It says in Psalm 35:27, *"The LORD be exalted, who delights in the well-being of his servant."* I love to bless my daughter with the desires of her heart and our heavenly Father delights in doing the same for us. We simply need to ask—and ask big!

If you don't have the vision for big blessings in your life that spill over into the lives of others, you will never ask God for big blessings. All that you see in the spirit, you can ask for with big faith.

5

FAITH AND FAVOR TO ASK BIG

It's easier to ask for big things when we have big faith and divine favor. Asking big starts when we allow God to grow our faith. And how does faith grow? *"Faith comes by hearing, and hearing by the word of God"* (Romans 10:17 NKJV).

As we expose ourselves to the written Word of God (the Bible) and receive God's revealed (*rhema*) words, which always line up with His written Word, we get what I like to call a "faith lift." The words that we hear and read have a major impact on our faith level.

Just as the words of the Lord increase our faith, the words of the devil decrease our faith and stir up doubt, which erodes our faith even further. That's why we must be careful what we listen to. A tiny bit of gossip, slander, or any other type of ungodly speech can seep into our hearts and tear down our spirits.

On the other hand, we can never have too much of the Word in us. When we get full from eating food in the natural, we often keep on eating when we should show some self-restraint and stop. When it comes to the Word of God, the opposite is often true: we take a little "nibble," then push away our "plate" (the Bible) as though we were full. We should devour the Word hungrily rather than pretend we're full after just a little taste.

We can never have too much of God's Word in us. Keep feeding on the Word and your faith will grow. Anyone else need a "faith lift" today?

ROCK-SOLID FAITH

Jesus wants us to have rock-solid faith. The key is knowing His Word and living according to it. Jesus said:

> *Therefore everyone who hears these words of mine and puts them into practice is like a wise man who built his house on the rock. The rain came down, the streams rose, and the winds blew and beat against that house; yet it did not fall, because it had its foundation on the rock.* (Matthew 7:24–25)

A rock-solid foundation of the Word gives us a platform of faith that is able to thrust us into a lifestyle of asking and expecting big things from God. When we ask big, we will see God do big things in us, through us, and for us.

Are you ready to go to the next level? God's ready to take you there; you simply need to ask for it.

DON'T MISS THE NEXT LEVEL

Whenever God is about to do something big in our lives, there is always a chance we will miss it. Such was the case with the prophet Elisha, who ultimately received the prophetic mantle of his mentor, Elijah.

When the LORD was about to take Elijah up to heaven in a whirl-
wind, Elijah and Elisha were on their way from Gilgal. Elijah said
to Elisha, "Stay here; the LORD has sent me to Bethel." But Elisha
said, "As surely as the LORD lives and as you live, I will not leave
you." So they went down to Bethel.   (2 Kings 2:1–2)

The Lord was about to take Elijah home to heaven. Elisha, who had served Elijah faithfully, easily could have missed what was about to happen. Even the prophet Elijah himself encouraged Elisha to stay at a certain place, letting Elisha know that he didn't have to go down to Bethel with him.

As the prophet Elijah went to Bethel, then to Jericho, and then, finally, to the Jordan, Elisha had three opportunities to go his own way rather than remain with his mentor. He had three opportunities to miss what God was about to do. And Elisha had three opportunities to miss the impartation of the prophetic mantle that would take him all the way to the next level.

Don't miss what God is about to do in your life and through your life. Don't miss the next level by failing to qualify. Elisha qualified because he refused to stop short of going all the way. Elisha paid the price by inconveniencing himself in order to serve the prophet Elijah until the end of Elijah's appointment on earth.

Are you about to stop before you reach Bethel because you are tired and weary? Are you about to camp out at Jericho before you make it to the Jordan? You must keep the fire of faith burning and keep on asking big—your arrival at the next level depends upon it. Now is not the time to pull over at "a rest area" or make "a pit stop" where the Lord has not called you to pause. This is the time for you to buckle your seat belt, fuel the fire of your faith with a full oil supply, and get ready for takeoff.

Elijah took his cloak, rolled it up and struck the water with it. The
water divided to the right and to the left, and the two of them [Elijah
and Elisha] crossed over on dry ground.   (2 Kings 2:8)

You are about to cross over, so hang on. The best is yet to come. All that you have been promised, and all that you have waited for, is about to unfold. All the years, all the prayers, all the serving, all the obedience—it's about to pay off.

EXPECT A DOUBLE-PORTION BLESSING

When they had crossed, Elijah said to Elisha, "Tell me, what can I do for you before I am taken from you?" "Let me inherit a double portion of your spirit," Elisha replied. "You have asked a difficult thing," Elijah said, "yet if you see me when I am taken from you, it will be yours…"   (2 Kings 2:9–10)

> TOO OFTEN,
> WE GET OUT OF GOD'S WILL BY
> FAILING TO GO ALL THE WAY.

After Elisha went the distance and crossed the Jordan River with the prophet Elijah, he was able to make his request for a double portion of Elijah's anointing. When we cross over with God to the next level, we can ask whatever we want and it will be granted to us.

Let's not be hesitant or timid in our requests. Elijah conceded that Elisha's request was "difficult"—but not impossible. Remember, with God, nothing is impossible.

As they were walking along and talking together, suddenly a chariot of fire and horses of fire appeared and separated the two of them, and Elijah went up to heaven in a whirlwind.…Elisha then picked up Elijah's cloak that had fallen from him and went back and stood on the bank of the Jordan. He took the cloak that had fallen from Elijah and struck the water with it. "Where now is the LORD, the God of Elijah?" he asked. When he struck the water, it divided to the right and to the left, and he crossed over. The company of the prophets from Jericho, who were watching, said, "The spirit of Elijah is resting

*on Elisha." And they went to meet him and bowed to the ground
before him.* (2 Kings 2:11, 13–15)

We must determine to go all the way, as Elisha did. Too often, we
get out of God's will by failing to go all the way. That's when we find
ourselves standing in the way of God and His wonderful plans for us. Be
determined to get out of God's way and stand in His will as you expect
a double-portion blessing from Him.

THE IRREVOCABLE FAVOR OF GOD

One evening, the Lord woke me up in the middle of the night and
said to me, "The favor of God is irrevocable." I had never heard that
before and I wasn't exactly sure what God meant, but I knew He was
trying to get a major point across to me. I kept praying throughout the
night and God gradually unpacked the revelation.

According to *Webster's New World College Dictionary*, something
that's *irrevocable* "cannot be revoked, recalled, or undone; [it is] unal-
terable." When the favor of God is on your life, no one and nothing can
alter it. And when you know you have the irrevocable favor of God, your
faith to ask and expect big things grows exponentially.

Joseph had the favor of God on his life. His brothers disliked this
fact and tried to change it, but their efforts were ultimately in vain. They
stripped him of the coat that his father, Jacob, had given to him and sold
him into slavery. For a short time, it looked as though the brothers had
stripped Joseph of God's favor. Yet they could not strip him of what
was given to him by his heavenly Father: his mantle, his calling, or his
dream. Whether his brothers accepted it or not, Joseph was covered
with the favor of God.

After being sold into slavery, Joseph ended up at the palace of
Potiphar, a ruler in Egypt. It wasn't long before Joseph's divine favor
caused him to stand out and rise through the ranks.

*The LORD was with Joseph so that he prospered, and he lived in the
house of his Egyptian master. When his master saw that the LORD*

was with him and that the LORD gave him success in everything
he did, Joseph found favor in his eyes and became his attendant.
Potiphar put him in charge of his household, and he entrusted to his
care everything he owned.   (Genesis 39:2–4)

Later, after Joseph correctly interpreted a dream for the pharaoh,
the pharaoh gave Joseph his signet ring, fine linen robes, a gold chain,
and more. He put Joseph in command of the land of Egypt. (See Genesis
41:41–43.)

The favor of God on Joseph's life was not only irrevocable; it grew
exponentially. Because of Joseph's upstanding character, that which
his brothers had taken from him—his colorful robe, a gift from his
father—was given back to him exponentially as *"robes of fine linen"* from
the pharaoh himself.

When the Lord is with us, we can't help but prosper. When we have
the Lord's favor, we thrive, flourish, and succeed at whatever we set our
hands to. No matter who may try to revoke the favor of God on our
lives, he will not succeed. When God's favor is on us, no situation, no
circumstance, and no person can hinder or revoke it.

Favor begins with a right relationship with the Lord. As it says
in the Bible, *"The fear of the LORD is the beginning of wisdom"* (Psalm
111:10), and *"those who find [wisdom] find life and receive favor from the*
LORD" (Proverbs 8:35). When we have a proper reference and seek Him
and His wisdom above all other things, we will receive His favor.

Promotion comes from the Lord, not from man. (See Psalm 75:7.)
Yes, God may use a man or a woman to promote you, but ultimately, the
hand that did the real promoting was God's. As it says in the Bible, *"The*
king's heart is in the hand of the LORD....He turns it wherever He wishes"
(Proverbs 21:1 NKJV).

There are four important keys to favor: *where, when, what,* and *why.*
In order to maximize our favor, we have to be in the right place at the
right time, doing the right thing with the right heart motives.

UPRIGHT CHARACTER ATTRACTS GOD'S FAVOR

Joseph's character was flawless and impeccable. No matter what his adversaries did to harm him, he never spoke a negative word against them—not against his brothers, who tossed him in a pit and sold him into slavery, which ultimately landed him in prison, nor against Potiphar's wife, who made persistent attempts to seduce him.

It's in his refusal to give in to Potiphar's wife that we see Joseph's strong morals. Her seduction occurred shortly after Potiphar put Joseph in charge of everything under him.

> So Potiphar left everything he had in Joseph's care; with Joseph in charge, he did not concern himself with anything except the food he ate. Now Joseph was well-built and handsome, and after a while his master's wife took notice of Joseph and said, "Come to bed with me!" But he refused. "With me in charge," he told her, "my master does not concern himself with anything in the house; everything he owns he has entrusted to my care. No one is greater in this house than I am. My master has withheld nothing from me except you, because you are his wife. How then could I do such a wicked thing and sin against God?" And though she spoke to Joseph day after day, he refused to go to bed with her or even be with her.
>
> (Genesis 39:6–10)

Talk about character! Joseph refused to sin against his God and against the man in authority over him. Although Potiphar's wife tried to wear down Joseph's defenses and repeatedly attempted to catch him in a moment of weakness, Joseph stood strong in his character, in his commitment to the Lord, and in his allegiance to his boss.

Joseph fled temptation—literally. Here's how it went down when Potiphar's wife got really desperate for Joseph's affections:

> One day he went into the house to attend to his duties, and none of the household servants was inside. She caught him by his cloak and said, "Come to bed with me!" But he left his cloak in her hand and ran out of the house.
>
> (Genesis 39:11–12)

Joseph didn't give in to temptation or hang around it, thinking he was strong enough to resist it on his own. He was smart and got out of Dodge.

James 4:7 says, "*Submit yourselves, then, to God. Resist the devil, and he will flee from you.*" Because Joseph was submitted to the lordship of God his Father, he resisted the devil and the devil fled.

When we are serious about resisting the devil, we need to "flee" from tempting people and situations. If we expect God to do big things in us, through us, and for us, we must learn to flee when we find our path leading to a place that doesn't benefit anyone but the devil. We must flee ungodly conversations, ungodly situations, and ungodly circumstances, so the devil will take flight, too.

When faced with temptation, many people just cower and hide, hoping the devil will leave them alone. They don't realize that they must actively resist the devil's temptations while living a life submitted to the Lord. They must be responsible with the favor of God on their lives, protecting and sealing it by submitting to God and maintaining upright character.

Even when Potiphar's wife framed Joseph for attempted rape, landing him back in jail, he still didn't speak a word against her but patiently put up with his wrongful imprisonment. Joseph had so much favor in his life because he passed the test and demonstrated Christ-like character. No matter how lousy his circumstances were, he didn't allow unforgiveness or bitterness to take root in his heart, but kept his mouth shut and his heart right. Because he was responsible to guard his heart, despite a long series of painful situations, the blessing and favor of God remained on his life. Everywhere Joseph went, the Lord blessed him—even in the pit and in prison. Everything Joseph did, God breathed His favor upon it. Joseph was responsible only for keeping the garden of his heart pure and undefiled.

Our hearts and their "overflow"—what we say, what we do, and so forth—affect all that we do and all that we are. Proverbs 4:23 says, "*Above all else, guard your heart, for everything you do flows from it.*" We must guard our hearts so they won't get polluted by anger, bitterness, or unforgiveness. If we can learn to keep our hearts right and our mouths shut when others mistreat us, the irrevocable favor of God will lift us to the top, in spite of any hardship we may go through.

SELFLESSNESS SEALS OUR FAVOR

We have established that the favor of God is irrevocable and that favor begins with a right relationship with God. We also explored God's favor at work in the life of Joseph. Now let's take another look at Esther, another Bible character whose life exemplified the favor of God.

From the moment Esther arrived at the palace, she won favor with everyone. On the path to your destiny, there will be people with whom it's helpful to find favor. As long as you are in the right place at the right time, following the leading of the Holy Spirit, your path will intersect with those people whom you need to meet. And when you meet them, the favor of God on your life will cause them to respond favorably, even if they'd rather kick you to the curb. The favor of God is not only irrevocable, it's bigger and more powerful than the will of man.

Esther won the favor of Hegai, who was in charge of the harem, as well as everyone who saw her. And, ultimately, she won the favor of King Xerxes, too, becoming his queen. (See Esther 2:8–17.)

The irrevocable favor of God positioned Esther permanently in the king's palace. Only God could have done such a thing. When God wants to put you someplace, trust me, that's exactly where you are going. It may not be at the timing you had expected or hoped for, but rest assured, God's irrevocable favor will cause your big dreams and soaring visions to come to pass at His divinely appointed time.

THE IRRESISTIBLE FAVOR OF GOD

The favor of God is irresistible. King Xerxes could not have resisted Esther even if he'd wanted to. When you have the favor of God, you can't help but have the favor of man. And man can't help but extend favor to you because the favor of God is irresistible.

The psalmist prayed, *"May the favor of the Lord our God rest on us; establish the work of our hands for us—yes, establish the work of our hands"* (Psalm 90:17). God wants His favor to rest upon us. This verse begins with the word "may." I believe the Lord gives us free will to respond to and receive His favor. He won't contradict our wills. He will not force His favor upon us. In the same way, the foundation of His favor is a right relationship with the Lord, but He won't force us to serve Him. He won't force us to obey His leading and He won't force us to receive His favor.

Even so, divine favor is available to us—and it's ours for the asking.

Jesus said, *"Ask and it will be given to you; seek and you will find; knock and the door will be opened to you"* (Matthew 7:7). Favor is just waiting for us to ask, seek, and knock. Most of the time, God wants us to ask Him boldly for anything that will benefit His kingdom.

However, there have been seasons in my life when the Lord told me to stop asking Him for something. Once, the Lord led me to retreat from asking, right was when I was in need of a house. I had been asking Him incessantly for a new home, until the day the Lord said to me, "Stop asking me for your house. When it's the right time, I will let you know." I was shocked, but I realized I had become like a little girl driving her parents crazy on a road trip by continually asking from the backseat, "Are we there yet?"

After waiting many years for a new home, I was growing impatient. But when I heard the Lord's instructions, I finally chilled out. I stopped asking and started waiting.

Two years later, out of the blue, the Lord said to me, "Start looking for your new house in December." I was excited that the time had finally come, even though I wouldn't have chosen a winter month—especially the busiest winter month—for house hunting. Sure enough, the perfect house for me was put on the market in December. There was only one problem: two offers had been made on the house before I saw it for the first time.

Neither my real estate agent nor the sellers wanted to show the house to me. The sellers told me there was already a solid contract on the house and a second buyer lined up just in case that fell through. Seeing the house would only be a waste of time, they said. Even so, I kept thinking, *This is the perfect house for me!*

I kept praying until the day I received a phone call—the sellers were willing to show me the house! From the moment Destiny and I walked through the door, we knew this was the house for us. It had everything we'd ever wanted—and more.

Things began to move very quickly after that. Both of the contracts the sellers had counted on fell through and we closed on the house during the third week in March. Talk about a supernatural turn of events! We didn't even see the house until the end of December and then, suddenly, my dream was fulfilled. All my years of whining didn't cause my season of waiting to pass any quicker. I had asked God for the desire of my heart—a new home. He heard me and when the time had fully come, He fulfilled my desire.

It's important to know when to ask and how to ask, but also when to rest. Yes, favor is just waiting for us. We must rest in that truth. The favor of the Lord God on our lives is irrevocable and irresistible, and nobody can deny it.

> IT'S IMPORTANT TO KNOW WHEN TO ASK AND HOW TO ASK, BUT ALSO WHEN TO REST.

There have been other times when the Lord has had to keep nudging me to ask Him for something, often in relation to fundraising efforts for my ministry. On one occasion, I felt led by the Lord to call a certain local businessman and ask him to make a financial donation toward our outreach efforts. When I finally obeyed the Lord's leading and placed the call, I was shocked. The businessman said, "I've been waiting for you to call me. I have money for you."

I thought, *Are you kidding?* I had spent so much time getting up the nerve to call and ask, and God had already made a way for me. And He had gone before me in a bigger way than I had thought. I was going to ask for $500, but the businessman said, "I have a thousand-dollar check waiting for you." I thought to myself, *Oh, you of little faith.*

God wants His irrevocable, irresistible favor on our lives to grow and increase, as it did in the life of Jesus. (See Luke 2:52.) No matter what anyone else may say or do, that favor is irrevocable, and it boosts our faith to ask for big things from our great big God.

PART II:

OVERCOME
PERCEIVED LIMITATIONS

6

"I'M NOT QUALIFIED"

Maybe today, you're thinking, *God could never use me to do anything big.* Maybe you feel like a nobody. Maybe you believe you're not qualified to seize any kind of "land" due to a perceived lack on your part—a lack of sufficient experience, strength, age, and so forth.

Let me tell you, you're just the type of person God wants to use. He loves demonstrating His power and might by accomplishing big feats through weak, inexperienced, and unlikely people. Don't believe me? Let's see what the Bible has to say about some of our perceived shortcomings.

"I'M TOO SMALL/TOO WEAK"

In the book of Numbers, God told Moses to send some men to explore the land of Canaan, which He was giving to the Israelites. So these men, who were leaders of their tribes, went on an expedition. When they returned:

> They gave Moses this account: "We went into the land to which you sent us, and it does flow with milk and honey! Here is its fruit. But the people who live there are powerful, and the cities are fortified and very large...." Then Caleb silenced the people before Moses and said, "We should go up and take possession of the land, for we can certainly do it." But the men who had gone up with him said, "We can't attack those people; they are stronger than we are." And they spread among the Israelites a bad report about the land they had explored. They said, "The land we explored devours those living in it. All the people we saw there are of great size....We seemed like grasshoppers in our own eyes, and we looked the same to them."
>
> (Numbers 13:27–33)

It's a biblical principle that God does big things with small resources—including "small," weak, unqualified people who consider themselves to be nobodies. Read these encouraging words of Jesus from the gospel of Matthew:

> The kingdom of heaven is like a mustard seed, which a man took and planted in his field. Though it is the smallest of all seeds, yet when it grows, it is the largest of garden plants and becomes a tree, so that the birds come and perch in its branches.
>
> (Matthew 13:31–32)

In the above passage, the kingdom of heaven is compared to the smallest of seeds, still managing to produce big results. God is always using "little people" to do big things. Maybe you feel like you're the "smallest of the small." Guess what? You qualify as a top candidate for God to use. Do you feel like the least likely pick? Join the club. You are probably God's top pick.

As Paul wrote, *"God chose the foolish things of the world to shame the wise; God chose the weak things of the world to shame the strong"* (1 Corinthians 1:27). God delights in defying our expectations when it comes to choosing people to carry out His work. Trust me, I'm the least likely person for God to use to write books and run a TV ministry. Early on, I was so timid and insecure, I couldn't speak in front of a group of even four or five. You'd better get ready and expect God to shock you with His supernatural plans for you!

> GOD IS ALWAYS USING "LITTLE PEOPLE" TO DO BIG THINGS.

Maybe your "small" faith seems too small for you. But your small faith, entrusted to the hand of God with expectation, can move any mountain that may be staring you in the face today.

Returning to the metaphor of a mustard seed, Jesus said, *"If you have faith as small as a mustard seed, you can say to this mountain, 'Move from here to there,' and it will move. Nothing will be impossible for you"* (Matthew 17:20–21). So, you say you have "little faith"? Great news—nothing is impossible for you. God can use even the tiniest amount of faith, in the least qualified people, to produce supernatural results. He says nothing will be impossible for you. It sounds to me like He's placing His "super" on your natural.

DON'T DESPISE SMALL BEGINNINGS

The instructions God gives to us may not always make sense to our natural minds. He told Naaman to wash seven times in the Jordan River to be cured of leprosy. (See 2 Kings 5:10.) He told Joshua that the walls of Jericho would fall down after his men marched around the city seven times. (See Joshua 6:2–5.) More often than not, God's directives sound illogical. Even so, we must always walk in obedience, following His guidance.

I waited for many years before God opened the door for me to begin a television ministry. It happened at a time that made no sense at all to me. My husband had walked out the year before, leaving me as a single mom with a newborn baby at home. Every day, I was having to believe God for the provision of even the most basic supplies, such as disposable diapers and baby food. When God told me it was time to launch my television ministry, I could hardly believe it.

God's timing does not correspond to our timing. *"For my thoughts are not your thoughts, neither are your ways my ways,"* declares the LORD (Isaiah 55:8). I'm convinced that He does things the way He does so He will get all the glory. I call it the "great setup." God "sets us up" so we might grow in our faith and learn to trust Him more fully. He does things in such a way, and at such a time, that we couldn't try to take the credit, even if we wanted to.

It was very obvious to me, and to everyone around me, that it was God who had opened the door for my television ministry to begin. I was given prime-time air on a major Christian TV network that many large ministries would have been thrilled to secure. But it was my land and God gave it to me—the nameless single mom believing God daily for diapers and baby food.

I was also believing God daily for souls to bring to salvation. God saw my heart and He breathed on it, bringing my dreams to life and allowing me to begin taking the land in television.

TAKE ONE TINY STEP OF OBEDIENCE AT A TIME

The earliest episodes of our television program were filmed in the living room of my townhouse. I knew that royal blue was a good backdrop color—and that was the extent of my pertinent knowledge. I could teach and preach because I had been doing so for years, but TV ministry was a whole new experience. With my limited knowledge, I scraped together enough change to purchase my first backdrop—a royal blue bedsheet.

God was teaching me to listen to His voice, even if it meant swallowing my pride and starting from humble beginnings. I knew what it was that God had called me to do, but I had no idea how I was going to get there. It was then that the Lord revealed to me a great spiritual truth that I will never forget: we get to where we are going by taking one tiny step of obedience at a time.

As I listened to the Lord each day, taking one step of obedience to do what He was telling me to do, the call of God on my life continued to unfold. As I preached under the anointing of the Holy Spirit from my very own living room, many people were encouraged and even saved. With the blue bedsheet behind me and a rented pulpit in front of me, I managed to change lives, and God continued to bless my every step of obedience. We must never despise small beginnings, or we may be thwarted by a spirit of pride. The Bible warns us, *"Pride goes before destruction, a haughty spirit before a fall"* (Proverbs 16:18).

God has commanded us to take the land He has planned for us. What's holding us back from stepping forward in pursuit of our territory? Let's not succumb to the "small beginnings syndrome." Jesus Christ started His earthly ministry as a tiny, helpless infant. That didn't stop Him from becoming Savior of the world. When God is on your side, there's no limit to what you can accomplish, no matter how humble your beginnings.

"I'M TOO OLD"

Sometimes, feeling "outnumbered" can mean sensing you're past your prime, or beyond the age when a certain goal is appropriate. For some serious encouragement, look no further than the biblical account of Abraham and Sarah, then known as Abram and Sarai.

It all started with a set of "illogical" instructions God gave to Abraham when he was seventy-five years old:

Go from your country, your people and your father's household to the land I will show you. I will make you into a great nation, and I will bless you; I will make your name great, and you will be a

blessing. I will bless those who bless you, and whoever curses you I
will curse; and all peoples on earth will be blessed through you.

(Genesis 12:1–3)

God told Abraham that he would have an heir—a son—and his offspring would outnumber the stars in the sky. (See Genesis 15:4–5.) Wow! Despite his age, Abraham was going to be a father.

Initially, Abraham didn't doubt God's promises, but acted in obedience. *"Abram believed the* LORD, *and He credited it to him as righteousness"* (Genesis 15:6). After a while, though, Abraham and Sarah began to get restless. They weren't spring chickens—and after years of trying, they still hadn't conceived any children. So they took matters into their own hands. Sarah told her husband to sleep with her Egyptian slave, Hagar. (See Genesis 16:1–2.)

Trouble begins whenever we agree with what someone else says that is contrary to what the Lord has said. It was Sarah's "bright idea," but Abram agreed to it.

Never agree to do something against God's Word or divine instruction, even if the person who suggested it is very close to you. Stand on the Word and don't waver.

It's never our power or ability that makes things happen; it's the power of God at work within us. As it says in Zechariah 4:6, *"'Not by might nor by power, but by my Spirit,' says the* LORD *Almighty."* We must realize that we aren't able to "make things happen" on our own, no matter what our age or circumstances. Instead, big things start to happen when we rely fully on the power of the Holy Spirit.

Yes, it takes crazy faith to keep on standing on the promises of God when they sound too good to be true. It takes crazy faith to step out in obedience. But it's always worth it, as Abraham and Sarah finally discovered. In spite of their old age and their impatience, God made an unbelievably wonderful promise to them.

When Abram was ninety-nine years old, the LORD *appeared to him*
and said, "I am God Almighty; walk before me faithfully and be

blameless. Then I will make my covenant between me and you and will greatly increase your numbers." Abram fell facedown, and God said to him, "As for me, this is my covenant with you: You will be the father of many nations. No longer will you be called Abram; your name will be Abraham, for I have made you a father of many nations. I will make you very fruitful; I will make nations of you, and kings will come from you. I will establish my covenant as an everlasting covenant between me and you and your descendants after you for the generations to come, to be your God and the God of your descendants after you. The whole land of Canaan, where you now reside as a foreigner, I will give as an everlasting possession to you and your descendants after you; and I will be their God."

(Genesis 17:1–8)

Wow! Abraham was ninety-nine. He still had not fathered a child with his wife and God kept reiterating all that He was going to do in and through the two of them. Once God had elaborated on His promises and even changed Abraham's name, the call was bigger and more powerful than ever. God was telling him, "It isn't over; as a matter of fact, you haven't even gotten started." Usually, it's when we feel as if everything is over that God is getting ready to breathe His life into it.

The next words from God were pretty staggering.

God also said to Abraham, "As for Sarai your wife, you are no longer to call her Sarai; her name will be Sarah. I will bless her and will surely give you a son by her. I will bless her so that she will be the mother of nations; kings of peoples will come from her." Abraham fell facedown; he laughed and said to himself, "Will a son be born to a man a hundred years old? Will Sarah bear a child at the age of ninety?" And Abraham said to God, "If only Ishmael [Hagar's son] might live under your blessing!" Then God said, "Yes, but your wife Sarah will bear you a son, and you will call him Isaac. I will establish my covenant with him as an everlasting covenant for his descendants after him. And as for Ishmael, I have heard you: I will surely bless him; I will make him fruitful and will greatly increase his numbers. He will be the father of twelve rulers, and I will make him into a great nation. But my covenant I will establish with Isaac, whom Sarah will bear to you by this time next year."

(Genesis 17:15–21)

Abraham laughed, but God wasn't kidding! Sarah bore a son in her old age and God's promises to her and Abraham were completely fulfilled.

Like Abraham, we often want God to do things our way. We want God to bless what we have done on our own. Abraham basically said, "If only You could do all this through Ishmael, Lord, that would just make things a little easier." Abraham wanted God to bless his independent action—fathering a son, Ishmael—as opposed to what God wanted to do at His command.

But out of His awesome love, grace, and mercy, God even blesses our messes. God promised Abraham that He would surely bless Ishmael, yet His covenant would be established through Isaac.

If Sarah could birth a baby at the age of ninety, surely we're never too old to be used by the Lord. So, keep an open mind and a ready heart, and prepare to be used in big ways by your big God!

"I'M NOT WORTHY"

When my mother was two years old, her mother left unexpectedly. One day, she was there; the next day, she was gone, without even saying goodbye. As a result, the spirit of rejection took root in my mother's life; it became a generational curse that was passed down to me. Its effects were magnified by the loss of my father through divorce when I was in fourth grade, which made me feel unwanted and unworthy.

RECOGNIZING THE SPIRIT OF REJECTION

There are many ways in which a spirit of rejection can secure a stronghold in our lives. The spirit of rejection was the greatest "giant" that the enemy strategically built in my life during childhood, working primarily through a generational curse and my parents' divorce. While I was glad to see their fighting come to an end, I felt deeply rejected by my father. The root of rejection continued to grow in my life and the effects became increasingly evident.

I was extremely insecure, easily intimidated, and had low self-esteem. I can remember feeling so insecure that I could not bear to walk into a room full of people by myself. Due to a negative self-image, I couldn't receive a compliment without quickly changing the subject. I would actually dress in such a way as to avoid receiving compliments on my attire. And my greatest fear was speaking in front of people.

The devil is such a liar. He tried to snuff out the call of God on my life from the very beginning. He tried—but God gave me the victory once I discovered who I was in Him. In order to slay the spirit of rejection, I had to know—really know—who I was in Christ.

Our circumstances don't need to define us. The situations that surround us need not determine who we are. Other people's words, actions, and thoughts don't define who we are. Our identity and our potential are defined first and foremost by the Word of God.

Consider just one of many things God says about us in His Word:

I took you from the ends of the earth, from its farthest corners I called you. I said, "You are my servant"; I have chosen you and have not rejected you. So do not fear, for I am with you; do not be dismayed, for I am your God. I will strengthen you and help you; I will uphold you with my righteous right hand. (Isaiah 41:9–10)

What a powerful and encouraging passage of Scripture. Father God has chosen us and not rejected us. If other people reject us, it doesn't matter, because our heavenly Father has not rejected us. Quite the opposite—He's chosen us!

In order to defeat the spirit of rejection, I made a practice of declaring aloud, "I'm not rejected; I'm accepted. I'm accepted by Christ." As we speak the Word of truth aloud and meditate on it in our hearts, we renew our minds. Out with the old lies, in with the truth, and the giant of rejection will fall down, in the name of Jesus.

OVERCOMING "PERCEPTION DECEPTION"

The devil wants us to be susceptible to rejection, but the Lord wants us to be rejection-proof. Society today rejects us if we don't look a certain way, act according to a certain set of generally accepted "rules," or earn a certain income. Society tries to teach our children at an early age to reject those who don't wear name-brand clothes, who look different, or who speak differently.

When we know who we are in Christ, as we discover the unconditional love of God for us and acknowledge God's acceptance of us, we become rejection-proof. We have to know it in our heart and in our spirit, not just in our mind. This type of knowledge comes only by regular study of and meditation on God's Word, and time spent in God's presence through prayer and worship.

When we have been made rejection-proof by God and His Word, rejection can't penetrate our hearts and spirits. We are not affected by rejection, whether actual or perceived. We are protected from, resistant to, and unaffected by others' negative thoughts, words, and actions.

Both actual rejection and perceived rejection can hurt us deeply if we aren't rejection-proof.

THE DEVIL HAS A HEYDAY TRYING TO GET YOU TO FEEL REJECTED.

Jesus tells us that the devil *"was a murderer from the beginning, not holding to the truth, for there is no truth in him. When he lies, he speaks his native language, for he is a liar and the father of lies"* (John 8:44). The enemy delights in causing us to feel rejected. If he can't cause actual rejection to come our way, he'll attempt to mess with our perception so that we believe others have rejected us. I call this "perception rejection."

Imagine that you walk into a room filled with people—and no one speaks to you. Or perhaps you approach a group of people and get the sense that they were just talking about you. The devil has a heyday trying to get you to feel rejected. He starts waging a war in your mind with thoughts that come straight from the pit of hell. He's using perception deception. Don't fall for it! Renew your mind to the truth and the giant of perceived rejection will fall, never to rise again. You will surge forward into the limitless life that Christ has for you.

WEATHERING ACTUAL REJECTION

Although other people may reject us for various reasons, God never does. Remember, God says to us, *"I have chosen you and have not rejected you"* (Isaiah 41:9). Keeping this truth in mind gives us a clear perspective when we face the giant of rejection.

When others reject us, we must remember that their words and actions don't define who we are. In most cases, they actually define that person instead, giving us a clear picture of their true character. If there's someone in your life who continually speaks negatively to you and about you, most likely, his words reflect who he is inside—a miserable, hurt, angry person. The Bible says the mouth speaks out of the abundance of the heart. (See Matthew 12:34 NKJV; Luke 6:45 NKJV.)

Those who are constantly putting others down often do so because it makes them feel better about themselves—in other words, it's a method of self-medication for a negative self-image. Don't let someone else's giant of rejection become yours. Whatever the circumstances that have caused a seed of bitterness to be planted in others' hearts, their words and actions don't dictate your value or define your identity. God's Word alone defines who you are—His child, fearfully and wonderfully made in His image. (See Psalm 139:14.)

"I'M NOT 'GOOD' ENOUGH"

We read in the second chapter of Joshua about a prostitute named Rahab who helped the two spies Joshua sent to scope out Jericho and nearby lands. When the king of Jericho found out about the spies, he began searching for them. Rahab did not betray the spies but hid them in her home, covered for them, and ultimately helped them to escape unharmed.

God used Rahab, though she was a "worldly woman," to accomplish His work. The truth is, God can use anyone who has an ear to hear His voice. Rahab recognized that the Lord had given the land of Jericho to the Israelites and she decided to cooperate with God's plan. As a result, she and her family were spared when the Israelites took the city of Jericho.

Because of her bravery and obedience, Rahab's name is recorded in the great faith "hall of fame" in the eleventh chapter of Hebrews: *"By faith the prostitute Rahab, because she welcomed the spies, was not killed with those who were disobedient"* (Hebrews 11:31). James commended her, too, saying, *"Was not even Rahab the prostitute considered righteous for what she did when she gave lodging to the spies and sent them off in a different direction?"* (James 2:25).

Later in life, Rahab gave birth to Boaz, who became the kinsman-redeemer of Ruth and went down in history as a faithful, upright man of God. Even more amazing, Rahab and Boaz were direct ancestors of Jesus Christ. (See Matthew 1:5–6.)

Maybe you aren't a saint. Who among us is? The key to a limitless life is yielding to God and desiring to obey His voice. You don't have to be without sin in order for Him to use you. If that were the case, He wouldn't be able to use anyone. Don't let guilt or feelings of inadequacy keep you from fulfilling the wonderful plan God has for you. He wants to do big things in you and through you, if you'll only listen and cooperate.

QUALIFIED TO TAKE ALL THE LAND

The enemy wants to distract you with commotion so you won't reach your promotion or seize your land. He wants you to be so caught up in problems, pain, and puny thinking that you won't last long enough to see your day of victory. But you are smarter and stronger than that. Be determined to surge forward and take all the land that the Lord has ordained for you to have.

Let's try to think along these lines: *someone's going to write a best-seller—it might as well be me. Someone's going to get that promotion—it might as well be me. Someone's going to secure the best airtime—it might as well be me. Someone's going to receive God's favor—it might as well be me!*

The two spies Joshua sent to scope out the Promised Land reported back to him, *"The Lord has surely given the whole land into our hands; all the people are melting in fear because of us"* (Joshua 2:24). Don't allow emotional pains such as rejection or self-defeating thoughts prevent you from taking the land. When you're aware of your identity in Christ and secure in it, you have what it takes to seize all the land as your enemies melt away in fear.

7

"MY RESOURCES AREN'T SUFFICIENT"

When God calls you to take the land, it means all of the necessary provision is in place. All you must do is step out in obedience. Too many people talk themselves out of going all the way to the finish line to take the land the Lord has called them to take because they look at their natural resources or abilities and get discouraged.

When God called the children of Israel out of bondage in Egypt and ordered them to cross over into the Promised Land, all of the provision they needed was already in place. They couldn't see it; they couldn't touch it; they didn't know the details. But they trusted the Lord.

When we set out to cross over to the next level and take the land, we must trust that God's provision is already in place. If we could see it, touch it, or read the financial report ahead of time, it wouldn't take faith, would it?

Yes, God requires us to step out in faith, trusting Him to have His provision of resources in place. If we are going to go all the way, to surpass every limit, we have to know from day one that God's got this. The details have been worked out; the needs have been met; all we must do is step out in faith and obey the Lord's instructions. We must claim His promise: *"My God shall supply all your need according to His riches in glory by Christ Jesus"* (Philippians 4:19 NKJV).

YOU MUST SEE IT IN THE SPIRIT BEFORE IT MANIFESTS

After we have stepped out, God will allow us to see His provision manifested as we take one step at a time in obedience. We must "see it"—know it in our spirit through prayer—before God reveals the details of what and where His provision is.

When the manna from heaven fell for the children of Israel, they simply needed to pick it up. (See the sixteenth chapter of Exodus.) They had to get it at the time and in the manner that the Lord instructed them.

Financial provision is never a problem for those who are in the Father's will. It should not be a big issue in our minds because God always provides wherever He guides. So don't be afraid to think like God thinks—big! Expectation and determination must stay alive in your heart and mind if you are going to go all the way.

What is money to God? He owns it all. *"The earth is the LORD's, and everything in it, the world, and all who live in it"* (Psalm 24:1). Never make a decision according to finances alone. Instead, make every decision according to the leading of the Holy Spirit. God's provision is already in place; He's simply waiting for you to step out in obedience and determine to go all the way.

God's Word says, *"If you are willing and obedient, you will eat the good things from the land"* (Isaiah 1:19). Plenty of people are willing... until it comes to walking in obedience and carrying out the "illogical" instructions the Lord has given to them. People categorize God's prompt-ings as "illogical" when they can't wrap their minds around them—in other words, when the directions make no sense to their natural minds or seem impossible according to natural law. But Jesus assured us, "*With God all things are possible*" (Matthew 19:26). We must be willing and obedient.

Being willing to do something great for God is one thing, but being obedient to the Holy Spirit's promptings is quite another story, espe-cially when they take you far outside your comfort zone. But in order for us to *"eat the good things from the land,"* we must be both willing and obedient.

The enemy trips people up the most in the area of finances. No wonder Jesus addressed the topic of money more than almost any other issue He dealt with during His earthly ministry. We must trust God alone—not our bank accounts, our trust funds, or our investments. Even if it seems we have far too little, God makes our resources to be more than enough.

A LITTLE BECOMES A LOT

Throughout the Bible, God almost always does big things with small resources. He rarely does big things with plentiful resources. This means that the excuse, "I have so little," is never valid.

Oftentimes, we hold back on doing great things for God because we keep looking at what we don't have. "We don't have the money," we say, or "We don't have the workers we need," or "We don't have the time." None of that matters, if God is in the mix. The key is doing what God tells us to do, one step of obedience at a time. When we have a lot of resources at our disposal, we tend to not rely on God, and that's not a good position to be in. Let's stop looking at what we don't have and start using what we *do* have for the glory of God, all the while expecting Him to show up. And then, let's watch as miracles unfold.

This is exactly what Jesus did when He fed the five thousand men and unknown numbers of women and children. I'd like to look at this event in detail to show you some key steps to take, no matter what kind of resources you have.

LESSONS IN MULTIPLICATION

> *As evening approached, the disciples came to [Jesus] and said, "This is a remote place, and it's already getting late. Send the crowds away, so they can go to the villages and buy themselves some food." Jesus replied, "They do not need to go away. You give them something to eat." "We have here only five loaves of bread and two fish," they answered. "Bring them here to me," he said. And he directed the people to sit down on the grass. Taking the five loaves and the two fish and looking up to heaven, he gave thanks and broke the loaves. Then he gave them to the disciples, and the disciples gave them to the people.* (Matthew 14:15–19)

Let's stop right there. Most people would quit if they were in Jesus's situation. They would look at their resources—five loaves of bread and two fish to feed more than five thousand people?!—and become depressed, discouraged, and disheartened. They would feel sorry for themselves. They might even try to manipulate other people into giving them more resources.

But we are called to simply take what we have and then, as Jesus did, look to the Lord. Jesus looked up to heaven. Don't look down; just look up and hold your head high. This is where your faith and trust come in.

Next, Jesus gave thanks. It's crucial to thank God for what you do have. Stop complaining about what you don't have and start praising God for what you do have. A grateful heart is always a forerunner for an increase in blessings. If you aren't thankful for what you have, why would you expect God to give you more?

Finally, Jesus took a step of faith because He expected His Father to show up. Although He had only five loaves of bread and two fish, He started distributing that food to the crowd—now, that was a step of faith. When we take a step of faith and just start doing what we know we should do, the necessary provision will always be there.

What happened next?

They all ate and were satisfied, and the disciples picked up twelve baskets of broken pieces that were left over. The number of those who ate was about five thousand men, besides women and children.

(Matthew 14:20–21)

"They all ate"—all five thousand men, plus the women and children who were with them. Not only did they all eat, but they *"were satisfied."* There were even twelve basketfuls of food left over. They didn't just get a little appetizer. No one left hungry.

Throughout the Bible, God does big things with small resources. Rarely does He do big things with big resources.

Father God wants you to take what you have, look to Him, offer thanksgiving, and then take a step of faith as you walk in expectation of His power to show up.

DON'T LOOK WITH YOUR NATURAL EYES ALONE

Are you looking at your scant resources and allowing the enemy to intimidate you? Intimidation and fear, grounded in our sensory perception of our natural circumstances, stifle all expectation for the supernatural intervention of the hand of God. But expectation fuels the supernatural. All you need is faith the size of a mustard seed. (See Matthew 17:20.)

Remember, God loves to use small things, frail people, and limited resources to accomplish big feats. He delights in using a little to produce a lot. Don't look at the little you have and allow the enemy to steal your hopeful expectation. When you give your small resources over to God, you can expect big results. When God is in the midst of your plans, the results are always big, powerful, and supernatural. All you have to do is keep expectation alive in your heart. Are you expecting God to do big things in you, through you, and for you?

THE NECESSITY OF EXPECTATION

Expectation is powerful. It can work powerfully for you, but it can work just as powerfully against you if you are plagued by negative thinking and low expectations based on the scarcity of your resources. Yet when you maintain God-inspired expectation, you can usher in the supernatural.

> *Since you have been raised to new life with Christ, set your sights on the realities of heaven, where Christ sits in the place of honor at God's right hand. Think about the things of heaven, not the things of earth.* (Colossians 3:1–2 NLT)

Another Bible translation says, *"Let heaven fill your thoughts; don't spend your time worrying about things down here"* (Colossians 3:2 TLB). When you fill your thoughts with heaven, your mind is filled with God-inspired expectations that line up with His Word.

EXPECT BIG AND BOLDLY

God wants us to expect big and ask boldly of Him, confident of His ability and willingness to grant our requests above and beyond our greatest dreams. *"Let us therefore come boldly to the throne of grace, that we may obtain mercy and find grace to help in time of need"* (Hebrews 4:16 NKJV). We wouldn't ask boldly if we weren't expecting a favorable response. But God assures us that His promises and His provision are ours for the asking.

> *And we are confident that [God] hears us whenever we ask him for anything that pleases him. And since we know he hears us when we make our requests, we also know that he will give us what we ask for.* (1 John 5:14–15 NLT)

Perhaps you need to raise your level of expectation today. God wants to release the supernatural in you, for you, and through you. He wants to transform your scant resources into incredible riches, but you have to expect Him to do so.

Expect is defined as "to anticipate or look forward to the coming or occurrence of." Don't allow the enemy to dampen or destroy your anticipation, or sow seeds of pessimism and doubt in your heart. Many people are anticipating disaster, lack, sickness, or defeat. Don't anticipate or expect the negative; expect and anticipate the supernatural.

EXPECT VICTORY

Even if you feel less than equipped to win your battles, the truth is, you are already on the winning side. You are "*from God and have overcome them* [your enemies, including the devil], *because the one who is in you is greater than the one who is in the world*" (1 John 4:4). Always expect victory and success. The ultimate Victor is standing beside you and He always wins.

EXPECT REPAYMENT AND REPLENISHMENT

Expect to be repaid all that the enemy has stolen from you. Joel 2:25 says, "*I will repay you for the years the locusts have eaten.*" Don't look primarily to other people to repay you or replenish your resources.

When you turn to people, wanting them to repay you for the hurts and wounds you have suffered or the years you have lost, that's unforgiveness. No one but Christ can ever repay us for our losses. And when God repays us, He does so in a way that's exceedingly, abundantly above all we can think, ask, or imagine. He repays us with supernatural bonus interest. If we keep our mouths shut, our hearts right, and our expectation of repayment and replenishment aimed at Him, God will repay us more than we could ever dream.

> DON'T ANTICIPATE OR EXPECT THE NEGATIVE; EXPECT AND ANTICIPATE THE SUPERNATURAL.

FROM RUNNING OUT TO RUNNING OVER

The prophet Elisha ministered to a widow in a way that brought to life the importance of expecting God's wonderful provision.

> *The wife of a man from the company of the prophets cried out to Elisha, "Your servant my husband is dead, and you know that he revered the Lord. But now his creditor is coming to take my two boys as his slaves." Elisha replied to her, "How can I help you? Tell me, what do you have in your house?" "Your servant has nothing there at all," she said, "except a small jar of olive oil." Elisha said, "Go around and ask all your neighbors for empty jars. Don't ask for just a few."* (2 Kings 4:1–3)

The prophet was telling the widow to ask for and expect big things. Sometimes, when we find ourselves in a place of great need, we don't ask the Lord for a miracle. Or, if we do ask, we ask too small. We need to have limitless thinking. When we take the limits off our thinking, we can expect endless possibilities—without any limitations.

With God, we can never expect "too big." We can, however, expect "too small." That's what the widow did. Yet the Lord was telling this woman to prepare for a miracle. I believe He is telling you the same thing today. Prepare for your miracle—and prepare big!

Elisha told the widow not to ask for a few empty jars. In fact, it's clear she's to ask all of her neighbors for all of their empty jars.

When you are expecting a baby, you prepare. You decorate and furnish a room for a nursery, you childproof the house, you take prenatal vitamins, and so forth. We must prepare for our miracle by doing everything the Lord tells us to do. And the first instruction is to expect big.

After she gathered all of her neighbors' empty jars, Elisha told the widow to go inside her house and pour her oil into all of the jars, setting each one aside when it was filled.

> *She left him and shut the door behind her and her sons. They brought the jars to her and she kept pouring. When all the jars were full, she*

said to her son, "Bring me another one." But he replied, "There is not a jar left." Then the oil stopped flowing. She went and told the man of God, and he said, "Go, sell the oil and pay your debts. You and your sons can live on what is left." (2 Kings 4:5–7)

The widow was discouraged and distraught, but the prophet Elisha was expectant. We must stay around people who are expectant because God is making room for our miracle right now. Expect it! Expect big! The oil stopped flowing for the widow only because she ran out of empty jars. If she had a hundred or even a thousand more empty jars, there would have been enough oil to fill them all.

Let's not be like the people to whom James said, *"You do not have because you do not ask God"* (James 4:2). The more we expect, the bigger the miracle we can receive; we just need to trust God to come through for us, even when the resources we have seem insufficient or the instructions He gives sound illogical.

The truth is, we will never birth something that we aren't expecting. I expected my daughter, Destiny, for nine months before I birthed her. What are you expecting today? Are you expecting defeat? Are you expecting rejection? Or are you expecting God to show up and do something supernatural on your behalf? When you expect big things from God, you set the stage for God to place His "super" on your natural circumstances, resulting in a supernatural intervention from heaven.

Once again, you don't need ample resources to do big things for God. You need only to expect your big God to show up and show off with your little resources. When God is in the mix, your small resources are enough, because He's the God of more than enough.

KEEP EXPECTATION ALIVE

Joshua knew how to keep expectation alive. And it's a good thing, too, because the people he led were a bunch of Debbie Downers. God planted expectation in Joshua's heart by speaking to him prophetically concerning what He had already ordained for Joshua to have. The Lord told him his territory would extend from the desert to Lebanon and from the Euphrates River to the Mediterranean Sea. (See Joshua 1:3–4.) God was basically saying, "It's a done deal!" All Joshua had to do was take the first step of faith to set his foot on the land that the Lord was leading him to take.

Expectation compels us to step out in faith. Expectation carries us across the line between faith and action. Faith without works is dead, but faith combined with expectation launches us into action. Once we put our faith to work, fueled by hopeful expectation, great things come about by the hand of God and the power of the Holy Spirit, no matter how small our resources or how empty our bank account.

8

"I'M ALL ALONE IN THIS"

The circumstances and situations in our lives can change frequently and fast. They can change without notice or even a hint of warning. But God is the same yesterday, today, and forever. (See Hebrews 13:8.) People will come in and go out of our lives for various reasons, but God never leaves us or forsakes us. (See Deuteronomy 31:6, 8; Joshua 1:5; Hebrews 13:5.)

Change is rarely easy, but if we have some advance notice, and if we have the confidence that the author of the upcoming change is the Lord, it's easier to embrace a new season. When people depart from our lives unexpectedly, it makes for a difficult transition. If we believe that a person's departure from our lives was outside the will of God, it increases the pain during our transition. But no matter what the circumstances, it's comforting to keep in mind that God is always there. He never leaves us, so don't even consider walking away from Him during a painful time of transition in your life.

> THE ENEMY IS TRYING TO SEPARATE US FROM GOD AT THE TIME WHEN WE NEED HIM THE MOST.

When someone leaves us, whether through death, divorce, or another reason, we often blame the Lord. We have to realize that the enemy is trying to separate us from God at the time when we need Him the most. We shouldn't blame God; we must simply trust Him, especially when blind faith is required.

A close cousin of mine died at the age of seventeen. This event left me feeling extremely upset and disillusioned. I was also angry with God. I had come to Christ not long beforehand and was a relative "baby" in the faith. Therefore, I didn't understand how God could have allowed Robbie to die at such a young age.

It was then that the Lord ministered to me with this Scripture: *"Trust in the LORD with all your heart, and lean not on your own under-standing; in all your ways acknowledge Him, and He shall direct your paths"* (Proverbs 3:5–6 NKJV). I want to encourage you today: don't allow the enemy to get you on to a "crooked path" or a detour when you encounter a painful change of season that may leave you feeling all alone. Instead, be determined to press into God's presence and hear what the Lord wants to say to you in His Word during this difficult time. Remember, you are never alone!

The thirty-first chapter of Deuteronomy records an announcement Moses made to the children of Israel regarding an imminent change:

> I am now a hundred and twenty years old and I am no longer able to lead you. The LORD has said to me, "You shall not cross the Jordan." The LORD your God himself will cross over ahead of you. He will

*destroy these nations before you, and you will take possession of their
land. Joshua also will cross over ahead of you, as the LORD said....
Be strong and courageous. Do not be afraid or terrified because of
them, for the LORD your God goes with you; he will never leave you
nor forsake you.* (Deuteronomy 31:1–3, 6)

When Moses made this prophetic pronouncement, he encouraged
the people to stay focused on where they were going. During every season
of change, we must not lose sight of the land that we are going forward
to take. We must not lose hope simply because people are coming into
and going out of our lives. This presents a challenge for us because it's
hard not to construct limits in our minds when we find ourselves in a
season of change, especially if we prefer the status quo.

God spoke through Moses to assure His people that He had everything under control. The plan was still the same: they were going to
cross over into the Promised Land. They were going to see the fulfillment of their dreams and visions. They were going to receive the desires
of their hearts. Even though Moses was not going with them, God was
with them. If we remember that God is always with us—that He never
leaves us or forsakes us, even when other people do—we can maintain
limitless thinking and experience limitless living. You and God together
are always the majority, no matter how many may oppose you.

And the Lord didn't leave the Israelites leaderless. God crossing
over before them and He also elevated Joshua to a position of leadership. Joshua was part of God's provision of leadership for their new life.

God sometimes speaks to us prophetically about an upcoming
change. If we maintain a powerful prayer life, we may receive "breaking
news" from heaven so we aren't caught off guard by change. Oftentimes,
God gives me advance notice of things to come. It always smooths the
transition process and gives me a greater sense of preparedness for the
next season that God has planned for my life.

Are you facing a season of transition today? Do you feel alone on
your journey to take the land? Are unexpected changes throwing you
into a tailspin? Is your mind "shrinking" as limits are imposed on your

thinking? Do you feel alone in your battle, in your fight? If you answered "yes" to any of these questions, I have great news for you.

YOU ARE ON THE WINNING SIDE

If you cling to the truth that you are on the winning side, it will keep you focused on your finish line and ultimate goal, no matter how many times it may rain on your parade. I like to say, "It's not over until it's over, and it's not over until God and I win." I don't know if that's grammatically correct, but it gets my point across. If I'm with God, I'm on the winning side, no matter how things may look in the natural.

The book of Deuteronomy concludes with the death of Moses. The book of Joshua, which follows, begins with the new leader taking the reins. It opens with a prophetic word from the Lord to Joshua, giving him direction and comfort during a major transition. The first chapter of Joshua records God's command for Joshua to take the land, as well as His words of comfort and multiple promises. Two promises are recorded in Joshua 1:5: *"No one will be able to stand against you all the days of your life. As I was with Moses, so I will be with you; I will never leave you nor forsake you."*

Let's separate the two promises and summarize them in simpler terms:

1. No one will ever be able to defeat you.
2. God is always with you and will never abandon you.

This is enough good news to keep us going all the way to our own personal promised land. By keeping these two promises of God in mind, we can spark our limitless thinking and ultimately soar with limitless living.

Often, our problem is failing to focus on God's promises. Instead, we dwell on all the challenges and unexpected circumstances we face. But no matter what sort of opposition may come against us, we are on the winning side. No matter who may leave us or forsake us, God is always with us. Comfort yourself today with the promises in Joshua 1:5

and keep expecting big things from God as you cross over into all that the Lord has for you.

FORGIVE ANY WHO MAY OPPOSE AND ABANDON YOU

In my experience, the greatest opposition comes from "church folks"—not from people of the world, not from secular "heathen," but from the religious church folks. I say this not to get you stirred up and angry at any "church folks" who have hurt you or done you wrong. My goal is just the opposite. Actually, if something has been stirred up in you and you just recalled something that one of those "religious folks" did to hurt you, this is an indication that you may still be harboring unforgiveness in your heart toward that person.

"Not me," you may be saying. "I forgave that person a long time ago; I just can't forget what he did to me." If that was your reaction, you need to calm down, cool off, and get real. Go before the Lord and allow Him to search your heart, by the work of His Holy Spirit, to see if there is any unforgiveness present. Be open to the Holy Spirit if He shows you any "little" lingering trace that may be trying to hang on to.

Forgiveness is a choice. In many cases, when the hurt has been deep, we need to keep making the choice to forgive—week after week, month after month, and sometimes year after year. It's crucial that we keep making that choice for as long as it may take to truly forgive our offender.

We can't try to skim over it or sweep a transgression under the rug. The Word tells us that if we don't forgive others who have hurt us, the Father can't forgive us for our own sins. (See Matthew 6:15; Mark 11:26.) That's why I'm saying we must look at our hearts with all honesty and not be too quick to say, "Oh, I don't have any unforgiveness toward anyone."

To return to my original point: no matter where your opposition comes from, when God is on your side, you will always be victorious. Paul wrote, "*If God is for us, who can be against us?*" (Romans 8:31). God was for Joshua and the children of Israel, assuring them that no matter who or what might come against them, they would always win, as long as they obeyed His voice, followed His commands, and pressed forward to the place where they were supposed to go.

Joshua maintained his courage and his unfailing trust in God, even when others were pessimistic, calling themselves "grasshoppers" compared to their enemies. (See Numbers 13:31–33.) It's easy to get the "grasshopper" mentality when you come up against giants in your quest to take the land. That's why we need the mind of Christ. That's why we have to meditate on God's Word day and night. That's why we have to put on our full armor each day.

NEVER ALONE IN THE BATTLE

God's Word is truth. (See John 17:17.) When we know the truth, the truth sets us free from the lies of the enemy and the oppression that comes along with that. (See John 8:32.) Don't ever buy the enemy's lies. Know the truth and stand on it! The truth is, you are never alone in your battle. You *must* know and never forget that God fights with you. He even fights *for* you.

NEVER ALONE IN THE MIDST OF ILLNESS

Maybe today, you are in a fight for your very life. Battling an illness or a disease can be spiritually oppressive, physically draining, and emotionally overwhelming if you don't maintain the mind of Christ by meditating on the Word of God.

Several years ago, following my annual mammogram, I was asked to return to the hospital for additional testing. I had just returned home from an out-of-town funeral service for my brother, David, who died after a battle with cancer. I immediately recognized the enemy's scheme to attack me with fear and I determined to stand against it.

They kept me at the hospital for most of the day, calling me back from the waiting room every so often for additional tests. As time went on, I became a little nervous. I was *really* nervous as I laid on the table while a team of doctors stood over me, discussing my test results. My doctor ordered an ultrasound of my lymphoid area, which confirmed the presence of a knot. During this test of faith, God enabled me to experience the solitary, lonesome feeling one often gets while waiting expectantly for a miracle. The good news is, you are never alone.

The enemy will do whatever he can to make you believe things are worse than they actually are. He paints a picture of doom and gloom, attempting to get you to give up hope. But your God can handle any trick the enemy throws at you.

Throughout the Bible, God promises to never leave us or forsake us. He will never depart from you, desert you, or abandon you. He'll never renounce you or turn away from you.

> YOUR GOD CAN HANDLE ANY TRICK THE ENEMY THROWS AT YOU.

You are not alone. You never have been and you never will be. Don't allow the enemy to convince you otherwise.

NEVER ALONE, EVEN IN THE MIDST OF APPARENT ISOLATION

Another tactic of the enemy is to isolate you or at least cause you to *feel* isolated. You may be surrounded by people and still *feel* all alone if you buy the enemy's lies or build a wall around yourself. But when you recognize this impression as a deceptive lie from the pit of hell, you can combat it with the Word of truth.

Say this out loud: "I am not alone. The Lord is always with me. He will never leave me nor forsake me." Speak it aloud on a regular basis. Whenever the enemy whispers a lie to your mind, declare the Word of truth boldly. And keep saying it until it gets in your spirit and the warfare of lies subsides. Declare the Word daily. The Word works!

God will be with you to direct you, sustain you, and assure your success. That's the very reason the enemy tries to discourage you—to cause you to feel all alone, outnumbered, and defeated. The enemy knows you are not alone; he knows you have the God of the universe on your side. The enemy doesn't know everything, but he knows enough to realize

114 *LIMITLESS THINKING, LIMITLESS LIVING*

that the strength of the heavenly forces surrounding you far outweighs the wimpy little force he's trying to bring against you. If you don't give up, there's no way the enemy can win. Thus, his only hope is to intimidate you to the point that you throw in the towel and call it quits. That's the point behind the lie that you are all alone. If he can convince you that you're alone, he just might get you to give up.

God has created you to have fellowship first of all with Him and, second, with other believers. It's not good for man to be alone. (See Genesis 2:18.) As Christian believers, we must not forsake the assembling of ourselves. (See Hebrews 10:25 KJV.) We need to come together regularly to encourage, support, and build each other up—even more so now that the end is approaching.

GOD IS ALWAYS WITH YOU

It's great to have friends. It's good and necessary to engage in fellowship. But the people we love can't be with us at all times. The only One who can be with us always is God. When Jesus was about to leave the earth following His resurrection from death, He told His disciples that He needed to go and be with the Father, but that He would send them the Comforter—the Holy Spirit—so they would always have His presence with them. (See John 14.)

The Holy Spirit is omnipresent, meaning He is able to be with everyone, everywhere, at the same time. What an awesome truth! The Holy Spirit is the power of God fulfilling the will of the Father on the earth. He is right there with you today, as you read this book and as you stand in the midst of battle. You aren't alone. All heaven is on your side.

Not only is the Holy Spirit with those who believe, but He wants to be *in* them. Father God wants His children to be filled to overflowing with His power. That's what happens during the baptism of the Holy Spirit. You are literally filled to overflowing with the presence of God and it's an experience beyond description.

Jesus told His disciples about the Holy Spirit baptism:

Do not leave Jerusalem, but wait for the gift my Father promised, which you have heard me speak about. For John baptized with water, but in a few days you will be baptized with the Holy Spirit.

(Acts 1:4–5)

Later, the apostle Peter exhorted a group of believers to be baptized with the Holy Spirit:

Repent and be baptized, every one of you, in the name of Jesus Christ for the forgiveness of your sins. And you will receive the gift of the Holy Spirit. The promise is for you and your children and for all who are far off—for all whom the Lord our God will call.

(Acts 2:38–39)

The gift of the Holy Spirit is available to everyone, not just a few select people. The Lord calls all of His children to repent, be baptized in water, and receive the gift of the Holy Spirit, the Counselor who leads us and guides us into all truth. (See John 16:13.) The Holy Spirit is the Comforter who gives us peace, understanding, and wisdom, just to mention a few of His blessings.

Yes, we are to be baptized in water, but we are also to be baptized with the Holy Spirit. In the first chapter of the book of Acts, the disciples were told to "wait" for the gift the Father had promised them. Sometimes, we need to wait in God's presence before the Lord releases the gift of His Holy Spirit to us. We shouldn't be in a rush when we're in God's presence. We must wait patiently.

Wait on the Lord; *be of good courage, and He shall strengthen your heart; wait, I say, on the* Lord! (Psalm 27:14 NKJV)

The Lord *longs to be gracious to you; therefore he will rise up to show you compassion. For the* Lord *is a God of justice. Blessed are all who wait for him!* (Isaiah 30:18)

The LORD is good to those whose hope is in him, to the one who seeks him; it is good to wait quietly for the salvation of the LORD.
(Lamentations 3:25–26)

We consent to sit in the doctor's waiting room for what seems like hours, but we often don't want to wait in God's presence more than a few minutes. The best things are worth waiting for. Be patient as you wait for the Person of the Holy Spirit to fill you to overflowing. You will be glad you did.

Again Jesus said, "Peace be with you! As the Father has sent me, I am sending you." And with that he breathed on them and said, 'Receive the Holy Spirit." (John 20:21–22)

I believe the Lord is breathing on you and your situation today. You are not alone. The Holy Spirit is surrounding you this very moment. Receive the Lord's peace. Receive the gift of the Holy Spirit and always remember that you are not alone; the Person of the Holy Spirit is with you always.

WHEN YOU FEEL OUTNUMBERED, REMEMBER...

Sometimes, our fiery trials and other challenges are not just one thing, but many issues all at once. It's a little easier to deal with a solitary situation that presents a challenge, but when we face several challenges at the same time, it can be overwhelming.

Here are a few truths to keep in mind when we're tempted to feel outnumbered and defeated before the battle even gets going.

WITH GOD, LITTLE IS BIG

In the book of Judges, we read an amazing account of Gideon leading the Israelite army against the Midianites and the Amalekites. The Israelites were not favored to win and Gideon knew it. When God sent an angel to summon him to rise up and deliver Israel from the Midianites, Gideon responded meekly, *"Pardon me, my lord...but how can I save Israel? My clan is the weakest in Manasseh, and I am the least in my family"* (Judges 6:15). Yet the Lord replied, *"I will be with you, and you will strike down all the Midianites, leaving none alive"* (Judges 6:16).

Remember, when God is on your side, you form the majority, no matter how many may come against you. Maybe today, you feel as if all the "-ites" are coming against you at the same time. Maybe on top of all the other problems, you're getting "backbites," too.

When all the "-ites" were attacking, God gave Gideon a set of instructions that sounded completely illogical. But obedience to God's illogical instructions is often the key to a miracle.

> *The LORD said to Gideon, "You have too many men. I cannot deliver Midian into their hands, or Israel would boast against me, 'My own strength has saved me.' Now announce to the army, 'Anyone who trembles with fear may turn back and leave Mount Gilead.'" So twenty-two thousand men left, while ten thousand remained.*
>
> (Judges 7:2–3)

Talk about an unexpected message! When going into battle, it would seem desirable to muster the largest army possible. But when God is involved, little is big! Throughout the Scriptures, we see God doing big things with small resources, so that in all things, He gets the glory. If you are ever tempted to credit a victory to yourself or to your big, bad army, God may take you down a few notches before you cross over to victory.

When given the opportunity to leave, 69 percent of Gideon's men departed. Gideon probably felt pretty lousy. It hurts to realize that the people we think are with us actually aren't. But it's better to identify and weed out the weak links before the day of battle. It's all right if you have a few deserters. Thank goodness God often exposes disloyal people ahead of time. When folks walk out of your life, your ministry, or your business, just bless them as they leave. Some of them weren't really with you anyway.

You don't need a giant army or a big team. As long as your team is committed to the cause and to the Lord, God's power will suffice. You don't need a big group of intercessors, partners, or supporters. You just need a power group.

God Himself sifted Gideon's army. And He continued to do so, causing the size to dwindle further.

> But the LORD said to Gideon, "There are still too many men. Take them down to the water, and I will thin them out for you there. If I say, 'This one shall go with you,' he shall go; but if I say, 'This one shall not go with you,' he shall not go." (Judges 7:4)

The best teams consist of members handpicked by God. Let Him sift your supporters and show you who you can count on. What is God saying about this one or that one? Whatever the outcome, stay positive as you remember Who is doing the sifting.

God took Gideon's army, which started at a size of 22,000, and reduced it to only 300 men. Ultimately, less than 1 percent of the original army remained. God was setting Gideon up for his miracle, just as He is setting you up today for your miracle. Remember, little is big when God's in it.

"During that night the LORD said to Gideon, '**Get up**, go down against the camp, because I am going to give it into your hands'" (Judges 7:9). The first thing Gideon had to do was get up. He couldn't lead if he didn't do so. God was telling Gideon to get up because He was about to give him his miracle. If you don't get up, you can't go on, and if you don't go on, you can't lead.

God gives you a word to encourage you to get up and then He encourages you when you begin to waver and doubt, as Gideon did. God went on to tell Gideon, "*If you are afraid to attack, go down to the camp with your servant Purah and listen to what they are saying. Afterward, you will be encouraged to attack the camp*" (Judges 7:10–11).

Have you ever wavered with doubt and unbelief? Maybe you are wavering today. This is your word of encouragement to get up and lead: God is about to give you your miracle.

If you are fearful, God will give you a word of encouragement to keep on keeping on. It's going to take limitless thinking with the mind of Christ for you to keep moving forward when you have only 1 percent of your original army left. But with God, a little is a lot.

Let's see how things played out for Gideon and his "tiny" army.

Gideon arrived [at the Midianite camp] *just as a man was telling a friend his dream. "I had a dream," he was saying. "A round loaf of barley bread came tumbling into the Midianite camp. It struck the tent with such force that the tent overturned and collapsed." His friend responded, "This can be nothing other than the sword of Gideon son of Joash, the Israelite. God has given the Midianites and the whole camp into his hands." When Gideon heard the dream and its interpretation, he bowed down and worshiped. He returned to the camp of Israel and called out, "Get up! The LORD has given the Midianite camp into your hands."* (Judges 7:13–15)

When you get up, God will make your dream a reality. He will let you know everything you need to know, right when you need to know it, as long as you stay tuned in to His leading by the power of the Holy Spirit.

God did it for Gideon and He will do it for you. It wasn't Gideon's big army that won the battle. It was Gideon's big God.

Maybe you are fighting a battle with the smallest, puniest-looking army you have ever commanded. Maybe you are fighting with the scarcest resources you have ever had. Remember, it's not your big army that's going to win the battle, it's your big God!

Once again, the leader has to "get up," and then he can encourage everyone else to "get up." When you get a word from God, you will be encouraged to get up.

> REMEMBER, IT'S NOT YOUR BIG ARMY THAT'S GOING TO WIN THE BATTLE, IT'S YOUR BIG GOD!

Then you can help others get up. The Lord was telling Gideon to get up and lead because his victory was already a done deal. The Lord had already given the Midianite camp into Gideon's hands. Gideon simply had to get up and show up. When we show up on the battlefield, God will secure the victory He has promised us.

GOD EQUIPS THOSE WHO GET UP AND LEAD

Gideon made the choice to get up and lead. You and I need to make the same choice, no matter how many times we are knocked down and no matter how much the size of our army may shrink. We lead most effectively by example. Unless we "practice what we preach," our encouraging words will sound empty and insincere.

When Gideon led the Israelite army against their enemies, he told them:

Watch me…follow my lead. When I get to the edge of the camp, do exactly as I do. When I and all who are with me blow our trumpets, then from all around the camp blow yours and shout, "For the Lord and for Gideon." (Judges 7:17–18)

Gideon told his army to follow his lead, to do exactly what he did. As you make the decision to get up and lead by example, God will always give you the grace to stand in that place of leadership—that place of victory with a small yet supernaturally strong army.

Will you rise up and lead? When you have a mind-set of limitless thinking, you can have limitless living as your battle outcome. Gideon beat the Midianites in a big way. *"While each man held his position around the camp, all the Midianites ran, crying out as they fled"* (Judges 7:21).

Your destiny is the same as Gideon's: big, powerful victory! You must hold your position. If you just get up and stand, Father God will take care of the rest. The enemy will run away crying. God did it for Gideon, and He will do it for you.

9

"I'M NOT ANOINTED"

When I preached at my first weeklong revival many years ago, God taught me a valuable ministry lesson. I was speaking at a little Pentecostal church in Oklahoma and we had a packed house with about forty people in attendance. In the eighth pew from the front sat a little old man with his cane sticking out into the aisle. He stared at me for the duration of my message, his face drawn in a deep frown, his eyebrows scrunched so low that they almost touched his nose.

His scowl was rather distracting to me, a young, novice evangelist trying to focus on delivering my message. Back in my early days of ministry, I was very timid and insecure. This gentleman's demeanor only added to the pressure I was feeling.

When the service ended, this gentleman made his way forward to the pulpit. He still wore the same frown and furrowed brow that he'd maintained for my entire message. I hadn't even noticed him blink or break the intimidating stare that was aimed in my direction.

As he approached me, cane in hand, my first thought was, *This guy is going to hit me over the head!* I braced myself for an incoming blow of his cane. Still wearing the same facial expression, he opened his mouth, leaned on his cane, and, with wrinkled face and furrowed eyebrows, said, "Honey, I ain't never believed in them there women preachers!"

I immediately thought to myself, *No, are you serious? I couldn't tell a bit by your facial expression tonight.* As these responses rushed through my mind, I was still bracing myself for a significant cane blow to the head.

He continued, "Although I ain't never believed in them there women preachers, there's just something about you, honey. You just keep on preaching!" I couldn't have been more surprised by the unexpected affirmation.

I will never forget what the Lord spoke to me that night. God was showing me that no one can ever argue with the anointing. When you are anointed, everyone knows it. They may not like it, but they will never be able to argue with the fact that you are a carrier of God's anointing.

God's glory has carried me through every trial and challenge I have ever faced. When you carry the glory of God's presence, the glory carries you.

Are you a carrier of the glory? If so, the glory will carry you. Don't doubt it.

People ask me all the time if it has been hard to be a woman in ministry. I always tell them the truth: no! I never allowed my gender to be an issue. I just always make sure that I am filled to overflowing with God's anointing, because no one can argue with the anointing.

I have preached in just about every type of church there is. I've even preached in churches where they don't believe in women preachers. I just go where the Lord opens the door and I act as a carrier of His anointing. Maybe the people at these churches think I'm "only teaching" and not preaching. I don't know. But I'm my fiery, loud, Holy-Spirit-emboldened self wherever God sends me.

We can't be anointed if we aren't being ourselves, just as David couldn't be anointed as long as he was wearing Saul's armor instead of his own clothes. (See 1 Samuel 17:38–40.) When we become the vessels God has called and created us to be—when we are filled with His anointing—no one can argue with it.

KEEP THE FIRE OF THE ANOINTING BURNING

The kingdom of heaven will be like ten virgins who took their lamps and went out to meet the bridegroom. Five of them were foolish and five were wise. The foolish ones took their lamps but did not take any oil with them. The wise ones, however, took oil in jars along with their lamps. The bridegroom was a long time in coming, and they all became drowsy and fell asleep. At midnight the cry rang out: "Here's the bridegroom! Come out to meet him!" Then all the virgins woke up and trimmed their lamps. The foolish ones said to the wise, "Give us some of your oil; our lamps are going out." "No," they replied, "there may not be enough for both us and you. Instead, go to those who sell oil and buy some for yourselves." But while they were on their way to buy the oil, the bridegroom arrived. The virgins who were ready went in with him to the wedding banquet. And the door was shut. (Matthew 25:1–10)

In this parable from Jesus, the oil represents the anointing of the Holy Spirit, which we receive by hiding ourselves in the presence of the Lord. We tap into the anointing, or the Holy Spirit "oil supply," by staying in the presence of the Lord. When we have a powerful prayer life, our oil supply stays high. When we worship in the presence of the Lord, whether in private at home or in a corporate setting, such as at church, we get a download of oil from heaven. When we meditate on the Word of God in the presence of the Holy Spirit, our life's lamp becomes filled with the oil of God's presence.

How's your oil supply? Are you running a little low? If so, you need to run into the Lord's presence. Don't run low on oil; run to the arms of the Father and get your daily fill-up.

When we keep the fire of God burning in our lives every day, it fuels our fight. We have strength for the battle, we stay encouraged, and we can go all the way to possess the land. When our fire goes out—when we lose the anointing—our hope, tenacity, and relentless determination fade away.

TRIM YOUR WICK

The virgins in Jesus's parable took care of their lamps by trimming off the charred ends of their wicks and adding oil to the reservoirs. We must add oil to our lamps daily, filling up with the Lord, and we must also trim our "charred ends," cutting away the flesh in our lives and trimming off the things in our hearts that aren't pleasing to the Lord. If we don't trim our wicks, it hinders the fire of God from burning at maximum capacity.

Trimming our wicks is similar to pruning our "branches," which Jesus talked about in the gospel of John, saying, *"I am the true vine, and my Father is the gardener. He cuts off every branch in me that bears no fruit, while every branch that does bear fruit he prunes so that it will be even more fruitful"* (John 15:1–2). To keep the fire of the anointing burning in our lives, we must be vigilant about ridding ourselves of all fruitless habits, thoughts, words, and so forth.

TEND YOUR OWN LAMP

When Christ returns, each one of us will need to supply our own "oil." We can't rely on anyone else to supplement our anointing, or our lack thereof. Preparedness cannot be shared or transferred.

Ultimately, each one of us will stand alone before the Lord and give an account of our life. That's why it is very important to keep the fire of God burning in our hearts. And that simply isn't possible if we have no oil. The oil is combustible. The oil is what ignites the fire and keeps it burning. We must add oil to the "lamps" of our lives on a daily basis.

In the passage from Matthew, each virgin had to provide her own supply of oil. If the lamps were bright and the oil burned fast, the young women may have had to refill their lamps every fifteen minutes.

> EVERY FIFTEEN MINUTES, WE SHOULD TAKE A PRAISE BREAK AND REFILL OUR LAMPS.

I think that's a great rule of thumb. Every fifteen minutes, we should take a praise break and refill our lamps. As we keep our minds and hearts focused on the Lord throughout the day, we can get our fifteen-minute fill-ups.

DON'T QUENCH THE FIRE

Paul cautioned us, *"Do not quench the Spirit"* (1 Thessalonians 5:19). In other words, we must not extinguish the fire of the Holy Spirit.

What have we been allowing to put out our fire? What are the things, people, or situations that cause our flame to dwindle? They aren't worth it! We must surround ourselves with people, and involve ourselves in activities, that fan the flame of God in our lives.

I believe the fire of God has gone out in a lot of churches today because they've run out of oil. Why? Because people don't want to pay the price to have the oil of God's presence in their lives. We must pay the price of dying to the flesh through fasting, prayer, reading the Word, and worship.

The cry of my heart is, "Lord, let the fire fall!" May He let His fire fall in our hearts and in our homes, our churches, our communities, our nation, and the world.

THE ALL-SUFFICIENCY OF THE OIL

All we need is the oil of God's presence. It's truly sufficient to meet every need. When we have the presence of the Lord and the anointing He brings, everything else falls into place.

Years ago, when Destiny was little, I would sing, by faith, a song that made a declaration to that effect. My husband had just left me, and all I had was a tiny, little baby and a great, big God. I soon learned that He was all I needed.

One day, during my time of private worship, I heard that song and as I sang the lyrics, I thought to myself, *There are so many things I want and need right now.* I needed and wanted groceries, enough money to make my mortgage payment, and a slew of other things. So, to be honest before the Lord, I started singing, "Lord, You are all I *want to* want."

When we desire that the Lord and His presence be "all we want," we can step confidently into the place of knowing that He's all we will ever need. The oil of His presence will meet our every need. Don't be discouraged or distraught. Wait on God's direction, through His written Word and His words revealed by the Holy Spirit (His *rhema* words), spoken to you in the quiet place of His presence, and then follow His instructions. Maintain a mind-set of limitless thinking, and you will be ushered into your destination of limitless living by the Lord's supernatural favor.

BENEFITS OF THE FIRE

THE FIRE INSPIRES US

I love the story of Joseph in Genesis. Most of us can personally relate to parts of his experience. Joseph was called a "dreamer" because God spoke to Joseph about his future in his dreams, through God-inspired visions made possible by the anointing.

If God chooses to speak to us about our futures, He doesn't usually include all of the details up front because He wants us to stay focused on the finish line. He wants our God-given dreams and visions to fuel our faith. If it doesn't take faith to reach a destination, that destination isn't worth reaching.

> *Joseph had a dream, and when he told it to his brothers, they hated him all the more. He said to them, "Listen to this dream I had: We were binding sheaves of grain out in the field when suddenly my sheaf rose and stood upright, while your sheaves gathered around mine and bowed down to it." His brothers said to him, "Do you intend to reign over us? Will you actually rule us?" And they hated him all the more because of his dream and what he had said.*
>
> (Genesis 37:5–8)

Joseph was excited about what God had given to him. In his excitement, he shared his dream with his brothers. The news didn't go over very well. But Joseph was so excited that he didn't notice how much his brothers were bothered by his words, for he went on to tell them about a similar dream he'd had. (See Genesis 37:9.) If his brothers' initial reaction had really registered with Joseph, he probably would have kept the second dream to himself.

When we dwell in the secret place and receive the anointing of God, He will often give us insights into the future—visions of wonderful things to come. But that doesn't mean we should necessarily go around sharing them with everyone we meet.

God once told me that someone was going to buy me a new Lexus. In my natural mind, I thought, *Yeah, right!* But it actually happened in 2006. And when I went around sharing my testimony, some people were not happy for me. They were envious, just like Joseph's brothers.

So, we shouldn't tell everyone about our God-given dreams and visions. But how gracious is our God to inspire us in those ways! When we carry the anointing of God, it's enough to know that He's smiling along with us, excited to see our dreams reach fulfillment.

THE FIRE PURIFIES US

Joseph's brothers acted out with hearts of jealousy that led them to unrighteous actions against their own brother. When anyone hurts us, it's painful. But when it's our own family, whether biological or the family of God, it hurts even more.

The envy of Joseph's brothers compelled them to treat Joseph unjustly. With malicious intent, they sold him into slavery, then told their father he had been killed by a wild animal. (See Genesis 37:12–34.)

Sometimes, the bigger our dreams and the greater our anointing, the bigger our struggles and pains will be on the journey to fulfillment. Along the way, God wants to increase godly character in our lives.

> GOD HAS A PLAN AND HE WILL FULFILL IT, BUT HE'S NEVER IN A RUSH.

When God tests and challenges our humanness, our flesh, it is often a setup for us to go up. He sets us up in order to build us up and take us upward. When you and I endure hardships as Joseph did, we have an opportunity to refine our character, increase our faith, and draw closer to God.

I had the call of God on my life from my mother's womb, though I didn't realize it until my later teenage years. But I needed to be healed before I could cross over and see the fulfillment of God's call on my life.

As I waited for this healing process to take place, I came to understand that God is never in a hurry. He has a plan and He will fulfill it, but He's never in a rush. He's a God of divine order and meticulous planning.

It took the children of Israel forty years to pass through the wilderness and enter into the Promised Land. The journey could have been completed in eleven days, but due to their grumbling and complaining, it took forty years. The journey was so long that the men who were of military age when they left Egypt ultimately died in the wilderness, never reaching the land of promise, since they had disobeyed God. (See Joshua 5:6.) It's a sobering truth that disobedience can signal the end of our dreams, our visions, and even our lives.

The males who had been born in the wilderness needed to be circumcised before they could cross over into the Promised Land. *"After the whole nation had been circumcised, they remained where they were in the camp until they were healed"* (Joshua 5:8). The circumcision was a cutting away of the flesh. This process can symbolize what happens when we allow the Holy Spirit to excise the "flesh"—sins, worldly ways, selfish desires, and so forth—from our lives so we will be fully ready to cross over to the next level when God says it's time.

After the cutting away of the flesh through circumcision, the people had to remain right where they were until they were healed. That was the case for me and it may be your situation today. The Lord required me to be healed before I could cross over to the next level—my own promised land. Yes, God still used me, but I could not come into my full potential until I allowed the Holy Spirit to do a great work within me. I had to ask, and then allow, God to do big things in me. Then I had to sit back and wait patiently while He worked.

It was worth the wait. He did a big, dramatic healing in my life so He could use me to bring big, dramatic healing to others' lives. His healing in me was so big, I wrote a book about it—my first book, *Don't Quit in the Pit*. In it, I share my testimony in detail. By God's grace, I never quit in the "pit," but I submitted to His healing process, which took years. Now, I can ask and expect God to do big things *through* me.

Whatever stage of healing you find yourself in today, God can use you. None of us has it all together—and we won't until we get to heaven. But when we allow God to purify us and heal us continually, we can take the land He has ordained for us, living a life of unlimited kingdom advancement. There's nothing else like it!

THE FIRE FUELS US PAST OUR FEARS

God says to us through the prophet Isaiah, *"Do not fear, for I am with you; do not be dismayed, for I am your God"* (Isaiah 41:10). Fear and discouragement are some of the devil's favorite schemes to keep us living powerless lives of limitation. He tries to cripple us with fear—fear of rejection, fear of injury to our person or our reputation, and so forth.

But we know *"God has not given us a spirit of fear, but of power and of love and of a sound mind"* (2 Timothy 1:7 NKJV). The spirit of fear comes from the enemy, not God.

God has given us all power and all authority in the name of Jesus, who said to His disciples, *"I have given you authority to trample on snakes and scorpions and to **overcome all the power of the enemy**; nothing will harm you"* (Luke 10:19). We can't afford to throw away our power by accepting a spirit of fear from the pit of hell. Father God has given us power to overcome every adversity life has to offer and this power is augmented every time we hide ourselves in His presence, basking in the anointing of His Spirit.

Not only do we have the power of God, we also have love, because God is love. (See 1 John 4:8, 16.) Of course, the enemy likes to mess with our God-given need for love. If we shy away from giving or receiving love, for whatever reason, it leaves us feeling rejected, and we end up withdrawing into ourselves, being bound by a spirit of fear and isolation.

The fire of the Holy Spirit destroys these self-imposed walls, freeing us to love and be loved as we were meant to be.

In addition to His power and love, God has made provision for us to have sound minds. Even so, the devil tries to make his lies echo in our minds on a daily basis, whispering, "Nobody loves you," "You're all alone," "You don't have any friends," and so forth.

When we bask in the anointing and allow the fire of God's Spirit to fill us, it drives out all the devil's lies and replaces them with the truth about ourselves and our situation. We must fill our minds daily with the Word of God so the fire of God can fuel us past our fears into a life without limits.

THE FIRE GUIDES US

> By day the LORD went ahead of them [the Israelites] in a pillar of cloud to guide them on their way and by night in a pillar of fire to give them light, so that they could travel by day or night.
>
> (Exodus 13:21)

When Moses and the Israelites were traveling in the wilderness, God guided them in the form of a cloud by day and a pillar of fire by night. Similarly, the fire of God in our lives gives us guidance. In the night seasons of life, in the difficult times, God guides us by His fire.

We desperately need God's guidance in the area of relationships. Associating with or trusting the wrong people, or going to the wrong place, can cause major delays in our lives. These people and places may thwart our plans altogether. But the fire of God leads us and gives us discernment in our night seasons. The fire lights the way so we can clearly see and discern the right people, the right places, and the Lord's timing.

FAN THE FLAME AND LET IT SPREAD

The prophet Jeremiah likened the Word of God to fire in his bones that he could not contain. (See Jeremiah 20:9.) If we have the oil of God's presence, it keeps the fire burning in our lives. And when the fire of God consumes us, we live a life of limitless victory.

The fire of God's presence destroys obstacles and eliminates hindrances to our quest to take the land. "'Is not my word like fire,' declares the LORD, 'and like a hammer that breaks a rock in pieces?'" (Jeremiah 23:29). His fire breaks every chain of bondage.

We need to be "fire starters" who cause oil spills everywhere we go. If we are shopping, we should have an oil spill on aisle 9, or wherever there is a person in need of the oil of God's presence. As we allow our oil to spill over in the lives of other people, the fire of God can ignite within them. But if we ourselves don't have any oil, or if we have a very limited supply, we can't share our oil with the world around us.

We talked earlier about the importance of being baptized in the Holy Spirit. John the Baptist told those he was baptizing, *"I baptize you with water. But one who is more powerful than I will come, the straps of whose sandals I am not worthy to untie. He will baptize you **with the Holy Spirit and fire**"* (Luke 3:16). The Holy Spirit keeps the fire burning in our lives.

If you haven't been baptized in the Holy Spirit, seek the Lord and ask Him to fill you to overflowing. It's impossible to keep your fire burning and maintain your "oil supply" of the anointing without the power of the Holy Spirit operating in you, through you, and for you on a daily basis.

The priests of the Old Testament were told, *"The fire must be kept burning on the altar continuously; it must not go out"* (Leviticus 6:13). Our prayer times must be "hot and fiery." We have to keep the fire burning in our altar experiences with the Lord. Our time with the Lord in prayer and worship allows the fire of God to burn the junk out of our lives.

As we keep the fire burning in our own lives, we must also continually pour oil into the lives of those around us. We need to seek out and find those who are spiritually dry and those who don't know the Lord—they all need some of our oil. Let's ask God to fill us to overflowing with His Spirit, so we may possess a limitless supply of the anointing to empower us and others, too.

PART III:

OVERCOME SELF-IMPOSED LIMITATIONS

10

LACK OF COMMITMENT

God has called you to take the land He has ordained for you, and lead others to take the land in their own lives. In order to fulfill these callings, you must be determined to go all the way. It's easy enough to be a starter, but it's a lot more challenging to be a finisher. Finishing requires complete commitment.

Plenty of people may start a business, launch a ministry, or begin a journey toward the fulfillment of a prophetic word, but actually crossing the finish line and turning that God-given dream into a reality is a totally different story. There will be a million opportunities to quit along the way. Only if we remain committed to the vision and push past all limitations can we go all the way and see our project through to a beautiful completion.

THE COSTS AND BENEFITS OF COMMITMENT

Commitment and selfishness cannot coexist. When we have selfish motives and are led by self-centered desires, we can't commit to anything outside our comfort zones. But when we are committed, we realize we must press past our comfort zones to come into our potential zones.

> TRUE COMMITMENT COMPELS US TO KISS OUR COMFORT ZONES GOODBYE.

True commitment compels us to kiss our comfort zones goodbye. Your comfort zone is where you do what you want, when you want. It's all about what you want, what you think, and how you feel. But when you are committed to something beyond and bigger than yourself, you are willing to get outside your comfort zone and you reach your potential zone.

We need to be committed to the call of God on our lives and the vision of the ministry God has given us. We must be committed to our relationships—our "covenant connections," as I like to call them. And we must be committed to a strong work ethic.

These days, many people shy away from commitment. As a result, they miss out on all the blessings that result from true commitment.

COMMITMENT REQUIRES SELFLESSNESS

A great picture of commitment is found in the biblical character of Esther, a young orphan girl who went on to become queen and ultimately saved her people from certain destruction. But first, she had to undergo a year's worth of beauty treatments and compete with a host of other girls hoping to wed King Xerxes. (See Esther 2:12.)

Now, I can imagine that the competition was particularly intense. Girls can tend to be a little "catty" and this was the competition of a lifetime. After all, Esther and the other young women were competing to become royalty.

As a teenager, I participated in a state-wide beauty pageant. The experience was a real eye-opener. Most of the other girls were very cut-throat in their determination to win. I was there with a friend of mine and we just wanted a fun weekend of meeting the other girls from our state who qualified for the final round. But not everyone felt this way.

Ours was a small state competition, but Esther was competing for an important role. In spite of everything that was at stake, Esther was not selfishly motivated; she was only committed to excellence in fulfilling her God-given purpose. When it was her turn to go to the king, she didn't ask for anything special, only what her caretaker Hegai suggested. (See Esther 2:15.)

Esther won the favor of everyone she met and could have whatever she wanted. Yet she did not allow this to shake her commitment to exhibiting sound character and saving her people, the Jews, from death.

Without that character and commitment, Esther would have grabbed anything and everything she could get her hands on. I'm sure her rivals did because they were only committed to their own selfish gain and pushing their way to the top. But Esther was committed to the king's purpose and submitted to it. She trusted the wisdom of those in authority over her, such as Hegai, and didn't ask for anything extra. That's commitment!

Esther was committed to excellence, godly character, and fulfilling her purpose. That's what brought her to the palace and propelled her through the ranks to earn the king's favor.

Just like Esther, we must be committed to our God-given purpose. None of us will ever fulfill that purpose without pursuing it "on purpose." We must purposely pursue our purpose in the Lord. It's never going to just "happen."

COMMITMENT DEMANDS DISCIPLINE, DILIGENCE, AND DETERMINATION

In our society, many people don't like to make commitments. Commitments require discipline, diligence, and determination. To many, that sounds like too much work. But remember: to whom much is given, much will be required. (See Luke 12:48.) Either we reap the rewards and blessings of our commitment, or we forgo those blessings.

On the job, for instance, the hardest-working, most committed person will be at the top of the list for promotion—from God and, in principle, from man. The one who comes in early and stays late will be kept while others are being let go.

Yes, commitment requires discipline, diligence, and determination—three ingredients that are essential for success in anything we set out to do. These traits are especially important in fulfilling our commitments and seeing our projects through to completion.

COMMITMENT CALLS FOR RIGHT ATTITUDES AND SPEECH

A lack of commitment always gives way to grumbling and complaining, but a committed person doesn't focus on the flesh, only on the end product or ultimate goal.

When we grumble and complain, we give voice to our flesh. But when we speak and pray the Word of God over ourselves and our circumstances, all the way to the finish line, we can remain committed to, and compelled by, the Spirit of the Lord inside us.

THE COMMITMENT OF COVENANT

The ultimate commitment is a covenant. God has ordained for the establishment of relationships I like to call "covenant connections"— divinely arranged partnerships that will enable us to cross over to a place of limitless living in Christ. God is a covenant-making, covenant-keeping God, so it's no wonder that covenant connections are so important to Him.

Here's what the psalmist had to say about God's covenant-keeping nature:

He remembers his covenant forever, the promise he made, for a thousand generations, the covenant he made with Abraham, the oath he swore to Isaac. He confirmed it to Jacob as a decree, to Israel as an everlasting covenant: "To you I will give the land of Canaan as the portion you will inherit." (Psalm 105:8–11)

The dictionary defines a covenant as "a usually formal, solemn, and binding agreement; a written agreement or promise usually under seal between two or more parties especially for the performance of some action." By definition, covenants require a commitment from all parties involved.

God brings covenant connections into our lives that are directly related to our call and purpose. We must guard and strengthen our covenant connections with God and His people.

As much as God is a covenant-keeping God, the devil hates covenants that are made among God's people because there is great strength in unity. The Word tells us, *"Though one may be overpowered, two can defend themselves. A cord of three strands is not quickly broken"* (Ecclesiastes 4:12). There is definitely strength in numbers, especially when God is in their midst.

Where there is unity, God commands a blessing. (See Psalm 133:1–3.) And God's blessing and favor are keys to limitless living. When you have covenant-keeping people living and working together in unity, you experience the limitless living that God has ordained for you—big time!

COVENANTS WITH GOD VS. COVENANTS WITH MAN

Maybe other people have forgotten, or chosen to neglect, a covenant they made with you. Many people desire benefits of covenant but aren't willing to do the work required to hold up their end.

But our heavenly Father never forgets or breaks His covenants. They are everlasting; they stand through thick and thin, no matter what. We should strive to live in such a way that the same can be said of our covenants.

> OUR HEAVENLY FATHER NEVER FORGETS OR BREAKS HIS COVENANTS.

My definition of *covenant* is "your benefit at my expense." We should enter into every covenant with that mind-set because covenants are a serious commitment before the Lord. Unfortunately, many people form covenants while thinking, *My benefit at your expense.* That's not true covenant and it's why a lot of marriages end in divorce. Too many people enter into a marriage covenant and have no idea what it really means.

In a true covenant, both parties are ready to lay down their lives for each other; they are willing to pay any price and make any sacrifice needed to guard and protect the covenant connection.

THE PURPOSE OF COVENANT CONNECTIONS

Since God is the Creator of covenants, when we remain committed to our covenant connections, we reap divine blessings.

Our covenant connections themselves are designed to bless us. God ordains these relationships for our lives to help us cross over into our personal promised land and possess His promises. Covenant connections put us in the place where God wants us to be in order for us to fulfill His call and purposes for our lives.

Just as we need to discern the covenant connections the Father has planned for us, we also need to discern when a relationship is not from God. We don't have time to waste. Certain relationships may drain us emotionally, spiritually, mentally, or financially. These unhealthy, out-of-balance relationships aren't covenant connections.

Covenant connections are life-giving, edifying, and mutually beneficial relationships in which both parties operate with a mind-set that says, *Your benefit at my expense.*

We should resist comparing our covenant connections with anyone else's. I always say, "You don't need a lot of people to like you; you just need the right one." When you are in covenant with God, He will provide you with every human covenant connection you need.

Sometimes, our covenant connections don't look the way we thought they would. Sometimes, the people we consider to be covenant connections are nowhere to be found during our times of need. But God is faithful and He always has the right covenant connection waiting for us. That relationship may just look different from the way we envisioned it.

When Joshua was leading the children of Israel into the Promised Land, he sent out two spies who found themselves in desperate need of a covenant connection. (See Joshua 2.) A prostitute named Rahab was the covenant connection that the Lord ordained and strategically positioned for them. When it was time for these men to do the seemingly impossible, God gave them a "least likely" covenant connection to facilitate their escape into freedom, which ultimately enabled the Israelites to cross over into the Promised Land. God placed Rahab in the right place at the right time. Her home was literally a part of the very wall that Joshua's spies needed to scale.

And after Rahab blessed these spies with a miracle, she received a miraculous blessing of her own—her family was spared when the Israelites captured Jericho. Both parties were blessed by the covenant connection that God had supernaturally dropped into their laps.

Maybe the walls you need to scale seem too big and too overwhelming. What challenges are you facing in your quest to take the land and fulfill what God has given you a vision to do? Even when it seems impossible, even when you think you have no "connections," God will supernaturally and suddenly supply the right covenant connection, just as He did for Joshua's two spies. Just keep expecting those covenant connections and faithfully hold up your end of the covenant. God will take care of the rest.

A PICTURE OF COVENANT COMMITMENT

A beautiful example of covenant commitment is found in the biblical characters of Ruth and Boaz, whose story we read in the book of Ruth.

Ruth was a woman of rare commitment. She was committed to completing her God-given assignment and wholeheartedly devoted to her covenant connections, especially Naomi, the mother of her late husband, and her second husband, Boaz.

Take a moment to read the book of Ruth for the full story. (It isn't long, I promise.) Even after Ruth was left a widow, she made this declaration to her mother-in-law:

Where you go I will go, and where you stay I will stay. Your people will be my people and your God my God. Where you die I will die, and there I will be buried. May the LORD deal with me, be it ever so severely, if even death separates you and me. (Ruth 1:16–17)

Ruth never grumbled or complained about the price she had to pay for being faithful to her covenant connections. She wasn't focused on her own desires or personal agenda; no, she was committed to God's plan for her life.

Her commitment earned the notice of Boaz, a wealthy man of upstanding character. As a result, she received her "Boaz blessing" and ultimately became his wife.

God was setting Ruth up for her Boaz blessing, but He was also setting Boaz up for his blessing.

Her mother-in-law asked her, "Where did you glean today? Where did you work? Blessed be the man who took notice of you!"
(Ruth 2:19)

Boaz was blessed because he took notice of Ruth and allowed her to glean the crops in his fields. But before he received the ultimate blessing of her as his wife, he gave his kinsman the chance to marry her. (See Ruth 4:4–6.) Boaz was *"next in line"* (Ruth 4:4) and he ended up receiving the blessing of Ruth because the other man refused to help her. Boaz was willing to pay the price and take the responsibility of marrying Ruth, a widow. With commitment comes responsibility, but it is always well worth the price.

Sometimes, the person at the front of the line doesn't want to pay the price for the blessing. When the kinsman in line before Boaz said he could not be Ruth's guardian-redeemer because *"I might endanger my own estate"* (Ruth 4:6), what he meant was, *I won't do it.* He acted selfishly because he didn't want to take a risk. So, Boaz received the blessing of Ruth, while the other man missed his blessing.

We must be determined not to miss any of the blessings God has for us. If we aren't willing to pay the price for God's will, God always has someone else waiting in the wings who He will bless instead.

Don't be afraid of what it might cost you, for God's grace is always sufficient.

When you are in a covenant relationship with the King of Kings and Lord of Lords, when you stay committed to your God-given assignments and relationships, there is no limit to what God will do in you, through you, and for you.

11

DISTRACTEDNESS

We must remain fully focused on our finish line—the goal at hand. On the way to fulfilling our destiny, plenty of hindering spirits will try to distract and discourage us. We must handle these hindering spirits the same way Jesus did.

TAKE AUTHORITY OVER HINDERING SPIRITS

In Luke's gospel, Jesus was in the synagogue in Nazareth for the Sabbath and read this from Isaiah:

The Spirit of the Lord God is upon Me, because the Lord has anointed Me to preach good tidings to the poor; He has sent Me to heal the brokenhearted, to proclaim liberty to the captives, and the opening of the prison to those who are bound; to proclaim the acceptable year of the Lord. (Isaiah 61:1–2 NKJV)

Then Jesus told everyone in the synagogue, *"Today this scripture is fulfilled in your hearing"* (Luke 4:21). He knew they wanted Him to perform some miracles, so He said, *"No prophet is accepted in his hometown"* and cited a couple of examples from Scripture. (See Luke 4:24–27.)

All the people in the synagogue were furious when they heard this. They got up, drove him out of the town, and took [Jesus] to the brow of the hill on which the town was built, in order to throw him off the cliff. But he walked right through the crowd and went on his way. (Luke 4:28–30)

The things Jesus said and did stirred up anger within a lot of people. In their rage against Jesus, the people in this account drove Him out of their town and even tried to push Him off a cliff. But Jesus took authority over the hindering spirits that were trying to attack Him through the religious leaders of the town. He took His authority and *"went on his way."* He walked right through the crowd of opposition, He remained fully focused on the Father's business, and He kept on doing what the Father sent Him to do.

WE MUST MAINTAIN A FOCUS ON THE CALL GOD HAS PLACED ON OUR LIVES.

What sorts of "spirits" or forces are trying to hinder you today? How are you handling them? Are you caving in to pressure, or are you walking through the crowd of opposition by taking the authority that is yours in the name of Jesus and by the power of Jesus's blood?

Jesus remained focused on the fruit, not on the fight. We, too, must maintain a focus on the call God has placed on our lives, pushing past every person, situation, and hindering spirit that tries to thwart our progress.

KEEP JESUS AS YOUR FOCUS

When our focus is on the Lord, everything will be in balance. A primary key to limitless thinking and limitless living is keeping Jesus as our primary focus. If we lose that focus, our priorities shift out of order, our perspective becomes skewed, and we begin to encounter limits on our vision, our potential, and our "conquest" of land and souls for the kingdom.

When our focus strays from Jesus to something or someone else, we begin to doubt. When we focus on the natural realm—the storms of life, the "wind and rain"—we are likely to sink into despair, discouragement, and even depression. Remember, we are not alone as we journey through challenging circumstances. Jesus is *the author and finisher of our faith* (Hebrews 12:2 NKJV). He is the Creator of limitless thinking—and He's right there with us.

To get a better picture of what I'm talking about, let's explore the story of Peter walking on the water. Peter literally learned the principle of focus that day.

> Shortly before dawn Jesus went out to [the disciples], walking on the lake. When the disciples saw him walking on the lake, they were terrified. "It's a ghost," they said, and cried out in fear. But Jesus immediately said to them: "Take courage! It is I. Don't be afraid." "Lord, if it's you," Peter replied, "tell me to come to you on the water." "Come," he said. Then Peter got down out of the boat, walked on the water and came toward Jesus. But when he saw the wind, he was afraid and, beginning to sink, cried out, "Lord, save me!" Immediately Jesus reached out his hand and caught him. "You of little faith," he said, "why did you doubt?"
>
> (Matthew 14:25–31)

Have you ever noticed that it wasn't Jesus's idea for Peter to walk on the water? Rather, Peter demanded that Jesus summon him. I believe that Jesus knew Peter didn't have enough faith to walk on the water. The Lord will never ask us to do something we can't do or aren't ready to do.

Peter was not ready, but in his zeal, he came up with the "bright idea" that he could do what he saw Jesus doing.

Yes, Jesus said those who believe in Him can do even greater works than He did. (See John 14:12.) But are we ready to do those works? God alone knows.

Sometimes, the Lord asks us to get out of the boat and walk on the water, but we say, "I don't think now's the right time, Lord." Remember, the Lord will never ask us to do something we cannot do or that He has not equipped us to do. But He often requires us to venture outside our comfort zone in order to bring us into our potential zone.

At other times, we may be like Peter—filled with zeal and wanting to jump out of the boat, only to realize it was our own bright idea and not the Lord's. When this is the case—when we impulsively act outside the will or the timing of God—we may "sink" as we attempt to do what we see others doing. Just because we see someone else doing something doesn't mean it's God's will or God's time for us to do it. If Jesus isn't asking us to get out of the boat, we'd better sit back and drift awhile.

The Lord is unfailing in His faithfulness to us. Yes, God permitted Peter to walk on the water. And when Peter began to sink because he wavered in his focus, the Lord reached out His loving hand and rescued him. The Lord does the same thing for us today, even when we get ahead of His plans and pursue our own agenda instead of His.

We shouldn't get ahead of the Lord, nor should we lag behind Him. We shouldn't be like little children who constantly run ahead of their parents at the park or the grocery store, nor like those who must be dragged along because they would rather stay put or go a different way. The children who walk hand-in-hand with their parents, sticking by their side, are the ones who benefit from their parents' protection. In the same way, we need to walk hand-in-hand with our heavenly Father, keeping in step with His Spirit, remaining right by His side.

When it's God's will and time for us to get out of the boat, we'd better jump out, dressed in our Holy-Ghost-faith-filled life jacket, and run on that water! Timing is everything. When God says it's time and we're focused on Jesus above anything else, we will have all the faith we need to fuel our limitless thinking and our limitless water-walking experiences.

DON'T LET INTIMIDATION BLUR YOUR VISION

We must envision victory in the spirit before we will see it manifest in the natural. If we can't see it, we won't possess it. When David prepared to fight the giant Goliath, he saw victory. He didn't fall for intimidation because He knew God was on his side. When God is on our side, total and complete victory is the guaranteed outcome.

> *A champion named Goliath, who was from Gath, came out of the Philistine camp. His height was six cubits and a span [about nine feet nine inches]. He had a bronze helmet on his head and wore a coat of scale armor of bronze weighing five thousand shekels [about 125 pounds]; on his legs he wore bronze greaves, and a bronze javelin was slung on his back. His spear shaft was like a weaver's rod, and its iron point weighed six hundred shekels [about fifteen pounds]. His shield bearer went ahead of him.* (1 Samuel 17:4–7)

Goliath, the Philistines' "champion," bore that title only because he had not yet fought against the Lord Almighty. Anyone can win battles, but no one can ever defeat the God of Israel.

Goliath's size alone was enough to intimidate the Israelite army. When we consider how things appear in the natural, rather than viewing them in the spirit, our vision becomes blurred, our perception is skewed, and we are easily intimidated. The key is simply to pay more attention to the spiritual reality rather than the natural appearance, for our God is *"the God who gives life to the dead and calls into being things that were not"* (Romans 4:17). Keeping our focus in the spirit gives us a clear perspective.

> *Goliath stood and shouted to the ranks of Israel, "Why do you come out and line up for battle? Am I not a Philistine, and are you not the servants of Saul? Choose a man and have him come down to me. If*

*he is able to fight and kill me, we will become your subjects; but if I
overcome him and kill him, you will become our subjects and serve
us.”* (1 Samuel 17:8–9)

If we succumb to intimidation from the "giants" in our lives, we will
automatically be defeated. We won't even stand up and fight. They will
overtake us and we will become their slaves.

Let's stop being intimidated by giants. We are on the winning side,
so let's slay those giants by the power of the Holy Spirit. The enemy is
subject to us. He's under our feet and totally defeated when we exercise
our authority in the name of Jesus, by the power of the blood. And we
can do this only when we maintain an eternal perspective that acknowledges the ultimate victory of Christ our King.

*Then the Philistine said, "This day I defy the armies of Israel! Give
me a man and let us fight each other." On hearing the Philistine's
words, Saul and all the Israelites were dismayed and terrified.*
(1 Samuel 17:10–11)

The enemy doesn't have any new tricks. He can only try to catch us
off guard with old, overused tricks. Meanwhile, God has not given us a
spirit of fear, but one of power, love, and a sound mind. (See 2 Timothy
1:7 NKJV.) Don't surrender your "sound mind" to the enemy by allowing
his demonic spirit of fear to take root in your life.

If you are trying to withstand the enemy in your own strength, you
will easily fall into fear. But when you recognize whose battle it really
is and you know that all heaven is behind you, fear will flee. *"Resist the
devil, and he will flee from you"* (James 4:7). The pit of hell is the source
of any fear you feel. Resist the devil and his demonic spirit of fear. Stay
focused on the victory that God has prepared for you.

IGNORE THE DEVIL'S DISTRACTIONS

When we submit to the Lord's rebuilding process in our lives and
ask Him to let us help others rebuild, the enemy doesn't take it sitting
down. He goes on the offensive.

That's what happened when the enemy heard about Nehemiah's desire to help rebuild the walls of Jerusalem. Sanballat the Horonite and Tobiah, the Ammonite official, *"were very much disturbed that someone had come to promote the welfare of the Israelites"* (Nehemiah 2:10). So they tried to derail the project.

The enemy tries to get us so caught up in personal distractions, such as problems and pain, that we won't have any time or energy left to reach out and help others. That's why we must first ask God to do big things in us, such as healing, so we will be available and willing to ask Him to do big things through us.

GOD WILL GRANT US A HARVEST OF GREAT FRUIT WHEN WE ARE FAITHFUL TO PERSEVERE.

As we keep our eyes on the Lord and maintain a heart of compassion for others, we will stay available for advancing His kingdom purposes. We can keep thinking, asking, and expecting big, even in the midst of warfare.

Nehemiah never succumbed to the enemy's attempts to distract and discourage him from completing the task he set out to do. We must have the same tenacity! We need to stay focused on our God-given call, even when the enemy tries to intimidate us and discourage us. We need to keep asking big. God will grant us a harvest of great fruit when we are faithful to persevere.

The bigger we ask, the bigger the warfare is bound to be. Remember, though, the greater the battle, the greater the fruit. Keep on asking because God's got this!

Nehemiah started *"this good work"* of rebuilding Jerusalem's walls and Sanballat, Tobiah, and a third man, Geshem the Arab, got wind of it. (See Nehemiah 2:17–19.) *"They mocked and ridiculed us. 'What is this you are doing?' they asked. 'Are you rebelling against the king?'"* (Nehemiah 2:19).

It's no surprise that the enemy tried to attack Nehemiah with intimidation, ridicule, and mockery. Satan doesn't have any new tricks. He recycles the same old schemes to discourage us from thinking, asking, and expecting big. He knows his only hope is to impose limits on our thinking—because if we think big and ask big, it's a done deal.

Our heavenly Father owns it all and He is in control. Everything God has called and ordained us to do will come to pass. Yes, there will be warfare. Yes, the enemy will fight against us, opposing our progress with distractions and intimidation. But with God on our side, we will always win.

VIEW OPPOSITION AS OPPORTUNITY

One way to avoid losing heart and giving up hope in the face of adversity and intimidation is to remember that every instance of opposition is also an opportunity for advancement. It may be difficult to see things this way, especially if the enemy's forces are coming strong against you, but all opposition is an opportunity for refining your character, boosting your trust in God, growing your faith, and proving yourself fruitful in the kingdom of God.

Don't worry about a little opposition. Don't worry about a lot of opposition either! Just shake it off, focus forward, and keep on thinking, asking, and expecting big. Before you know it, big fruit will manifest as a direct result of your perseverance, just as it did for Nehemiah. Thanks to his faith, a lot of people came together to repair the city's walls. (See Nehemiah 3.)

> *But when Sanballat, Tobiah, the Arabs, the Ammonites and the people of Ashdod heard that the repairs to Jerusalem's walls had gone ahead and that the gaps were being closed, they were very angry. They all plotted together to come and fight against Jerusalem and stir up trouble against it. But we prayed to our God and posted a guard day and night to meet this threat.* (Nehemiah 4:7–9)

Nehemiah asked God to do big things through him, and it was a done deal. Yes, there were challenges and warfare ahead; nevertheless, the outcome had already been determined. God had already granted big fruit in the spirit.

STAND IN PRAYER

While Nehemiah was waiting for the results of his labor to manifest in the natural, he simply stood in prayer. Through prayer, he encouraged and strengthened himself and everyone else. Through prayer, the results were declared and the warfare was silenced.

As we continue to ask big in prayer, we will continually see big results manifested for kingdom purposes. God wants to use you to do big things for His kingdom even more than you want Him to do so. And so, after you have asked, you simply need to stand in prayer.

Encourage yourself in the Lord today. You have asked and God has granted it, even if you don't see it manifesting just yet. Remember, God's timing is perfect. *"There is a time for everything, and a season for every activity under the heavens"* (Ecclesiastes 3:1).

Jesus said:

You did not choose me, but I chose you and appointed you so that you might go and bear fruit—fruit that will last—and so that whatever you ask in my name the Father will give you." (John 15:16)

It's already been decided. God chose, appointed, and anointed you for the task you are undertaking. As a result, no one and nothing can hinder you from accomplishing the will of the Father. You passed your biggest test: you asked God to use you in a big way. You asked and He responded, just as He did for Nehemiah. No matter how many battles you face, you will always be victorious, so fear not. Don't be discouraged or get upset. God will finish what He started in you.

DENY THE ENEMY'S LIES

Nehemiah's struggles weren't over yet. His opponents continued to try to thwart his progress.

> *Sanballat and Geshem sent me this message: "Come, let us meet together in one of the villages on the plain of Ono." But they were scheming to harm me; so I sent messengers to them with this reply: "I am carrying on a great project and cannot go down. Why should the work stop while I leave it and go down to you?" Four times they sent me the same message, and each time I gave them the same answer.*
> (Nehemiah 6:2–4)

The enemy is always sending messages that are lies coming directly from the pit of hell. Don't believe his lies; stay focused on God's Word of truth. Believe me, the enemy wants to meet with you like he asked to meet with Nehemiah. In the middle of the night, he wants to torment you with his lies and intimidating thoughts. Satan will meet with you at any place, at any time, in his attempts to hinder the work you asked God to do through you.

Nehemiah refused to be distracted. He refused to take time away from the great project he was doing for God's people. He refused to put his work on hold to cater to the enemy. Time and time again, the enemy tried to "meet with" Nehemiah; time and time again, Nehemiah refused.

How will you react to the enemy's distractions? He's saying to himself, *Oh, no! He's completing the work! Oh, no! Her ministry for God is going forward!* Yes, the enemy wants to meet with you on the plain of Ono. He wants to distract you and stop you.

DON'T BEND UNDER PRESSURE

> *Then, the fifth time, Sanballat sent his aide to me with the same message, and in his hand was an unsealed letter in which was written: "It is reported among the nations—and Geshem says it is true—that you and the Jews are plotting to revolt, and therefore you are building the wall. Moreover, according to these reports you*

are about to become their king and have even appointed prophets to make this proclamation about you in Jerusalem: 'There is a king in Judah!' Now this report will get back to the king; so come, let us meet together." (Nehemiah 6:5–7)

Five times, the enemy sent the same message to Nehemiah. This time, he also threw in false accusations. I have to laugh when I read the phrase *"and Geshem says it is true."* Don't you love it when someone tries to come against you with the line, "Everyone is saying…"? Sanballat must have thought Geshem's opinion held sway. But no one died and left Geshem in charge of Nehemiah's life, so he didn't really give a hoot about what Geshem was saying, or whether it was true.

> WORRY AND FEAR WEAKEN YOU, BUT PRAYER STRENGTHENS YOU.

Our kids use this tactic sometimes. Destiny used to come home from school and say, "But everyone's is doing it, Mom!" I'd respond, "Not everyone is doing it, because *you* are not doing it. I don't care what everyone else is doing. I'm not everyone else's momma. I'm your momma, and I said you aren't doing it, so you aren't. Case dismissed!"

The enemy used some desperate tactics in his desire to stop Nehemiah and put an end to his work. But good old Nehemiah, he wasn't shaken or discouraged, and he didn't think about meeting with the enemy. Nehemiah remained focused. What a powerful example!

> *I sent him this reply: "Nothing like what you are saying is happening; you are just making it up out of your head." They were all trying to frighten us, thinking, "Their hands will get too weak for the work, and it will not be completed." But I prayed, "Now strengthen my hands."* (Nehemiah 6:8–9)

I love Nehemiah and his example to us, his heart, and his tenacity. Let's be finishers, not just starters. Let's complete the big work we asked

God to give us. And remember, worry and fear weaken you, but prayer strengthens you. Pray that God will strengthen your hands. You've already ask big and you've already stepped out in faith to do big; now, keep on praying with intense focus and allow God to strengthen your hands so you finish strong.

FOCUS ON THE FINISH LINE

When David came against the giant Goliath, he focused on the end result—victory for God's people. He wasn't fixated on the size or apparent strength of his opponent, or on what other people were saying. David knew who was with him—the Lord God Himself. And he knew Goliath was nothing to God. David knew he served a big, *big* God, who would do nothing less than deliver a big victory.

Let's look at the passage showing David's encounter with the giant.

> *David said to the Philistine, "You come against me with sword and spear and javelin, but I come against you in the name of the LORD Almighty, the God of the armies of Israel, whom you have defied. This day the LORD will deliver you into my hands, and I'll strike you down and cut off your head. This very day I will give the carcasses of the Philistine army to the birds and the wild animals, and the whole world will know that there is a God in Israel. All those gathered here will know that it is not by sword or spear that the LORD saves; for the battle is the LORD's, and he will give all of you into our hands."*
>
> (1 Samuel 17:45–47)

David didn't stress out; he just rested in the Lord. When you are filled with stress, you can't rest. But when you rest in the Lord, your victory over the giants you face is assured. You are too blessed to be stressed, so just rest.

God wants to fight your giants for you. He wants to defeat your giants supernaturally. God got all the glory the day Goliath was defeated, and He wants to get all the glory when He supernaturally slays your giants for you, too. The key is focusing on the finish line and letting God take care of the rest.

12

A DEFEATIST MIND-SET

Hope is a vital component of limitless thinking; with it, you stay determined to go all the way. We must hold on to hope if we expect to emerge victorious from a fight or a spiritual battle, or even a project we decide to undertake.

I like to think of the word *hope* as an acronym for "Holding On with Patient Expectation." We need patience because it may take a long time for what we're hoping for to occur. *"Let us not become weary in doing good, for at the proper time we will reap a harvest **if we do not give up**"* (Galatians 6:9). We must never give up, for at the proper time, we will see our God-given dreams coming to fruition.

> *The L*ORD *said to Moses, "Send some men to explore the land of Canaan, which I am giving to the Israelites. From each ancestral tribe send one of its leaders." So at the L*ORD's *command Moses sent them out from the Desert of Paran. All of them were leaders of the Israelites.* (Numbers 13:1–3)

But Moses had to deal with some doubters and naysayers in his pursuit of the Promised Land. As I mentioned earlier, the explorers came back with the report that although the land was flowing *"with milk and honey,"* the people who lived there were so large and powerful that the Israelites were *"like grasshoppers"* compared to them. (See Numbers 13:26–33.) But Caleb wasn't having any of that nonsense. He told the Israelites, *"We should go up and take possession of the land, for we can certainly do it"* (Numbers 13:30).

Caleb had a heart full of hope. He was confident in his army's ability to defeat the enemy. But most of the other men who'd been sent to scout out the land weren't as certain. They were quaking in their boots.

Along with Caleb, Joshua felt sure of God's presence and provision. The two of them told the Israelites:

> *The land we passed through and explored is exceedingly good. If the L*ORD *is pleased with us, he will lead us into that land, a land flowing with milk and honey, and will give it to us. Only do not rebel against the L*ORD. *And do not be afraid of the people of the land, because we will devour them. Their protection is gone, but the L*ORD *is with us. Do not be afraid of them.* (Numbers 14:7–9)

But the people didn't believe them and even talked about stoning Caleb and Joshua. God was so annoyed by their lack of faith, He destroyed all of the "doubting scouts." Only Caleb and Joshua survived. (See Numbers 14:36–38.)

FAITH FUELS YOUR FIGHT

Caleb and Joshua held on to hope because they were focused on the strength of their God, not on the apparent strength of their opponents.

What are you focused on today? If we fix our eyes on the problems and challenges of everyday life, we will talk ourselves out of going all the way to take the land. But if we fix our eyes on the Lord and seek Him daily, our victory will be within reach.

The Bible expresses it this way:

Let us run with perseverance the race marked out for us, fixing our eyes on Jesus, the pioneer and perfecter of faith. For the joy set before him he endured the cross, scorning its shame, and sat down at the right hand of the throne of God. Consider him who endured such opposition from sinners, so that you will not grow weary and lose heart. (Hebrews 12:1–3)

When we fix our eyes on the Lord, we won't grow weary in times of battle. Let the Perfecter of our faith fuel your fight to go all the way. As we focus on the Lord and keep Him as our source of hope, we won't grow weary when it's time to fight.

[God] *gives strength to the weary and increases the power of the weak. Even youths grow tired and weary, and young men stumble and fall; but those who hope in the LORD will renew their strength. They will soar on wings like eagles; they will run and not grow weary, they will walk and not be faint.* (Isaiah 40:29–31)

The Lord offers us a great deal in that passage! All we have to do is keep our hope in the Lord and we will reap all of those wonderful benefits. If your hope is in your paycheck, your retirement account, your greatest supporters, or the people you always thought you could count on, you'd better realign your source of hope.

When you hope in the Lord, He will:

+ Give you strength when you are weary
+ Increase your power when you are feeling weak
+ Renew your strength
+ Enable you to soar like an eagle

+ Help you run without getting tired
+ Cause you to walk through any situation without collapsing

I'm big on bargains. I love a good deal. Whenever God spells out blessings and promises in His Word, they are always exceptional deals. If you are even merely considering putting your hope in anything other than the Lord, you must realize that the devil is trying to rip you off. God has an amazing deal for you that you can't afford to pass up. Realign your source of hope today and enjoy the journey as you go all the way with the limitless lifestyle He paid the price for you to inherit.

GET OVER NEGATIVITY AND NAYSAYING

Those who think small will never cross over to the next level. We are required to think big if we expect to reach the next step. We need to set the stage for a big manifestation if we want to see one fulfilled before our eyes.

When it was God's appointed time for the children of Israel to cross over from bondage in Egypt into the freedom of the wilderness, they were required to think big. At the banks of the Red Sea, they were presented with a challenge: either think big and cross over, or think according to their natural, limited mind-set, stay put, and face recapture by Pharaoh's army.

> *As Pharaoh approached, the Israelites looked up, and there were the Egyptians, marching after them. They were terrified and cried out to the* Lord.…*Moses answered the people, "Do not be afraid. Stand firm and you will see the deliverance the* Lord *will bring you today. The Egyptians you see today you will never see again. The* Lord *will fight for you; you need only to be still." Then the* Lord *said to Moses, "Why are you crying out to me? Tell the Israelites to move on. Raise your staff and stretch out your hand over the sea to divide the water so that the Israelites can go through the sea on dry ground. I will harden the hearts of the Egyptians so that they will go in after them. And I will gain glory through Pharaoh and all his army, through his chariots and his horsemen. The Egyptians will know*

that I am the LORD.*"…Then Moses stretched out his hand over the sea, and all that night the* LORD *drove the sea back with a strong east wind and turned it into dry land. The waters were divided, and the Israelites went through the sea on dry ground, with a wall of water on their right and on their left. The Egyptians pursued them, and all Pharaoh's horses and chariots and horsemen followed them into the sea.…The* LORD *looked down…at the Egyptian army and threw it into confusion. He jammed the wheels of their chariots so that they had difficulty driving. And the Egyptians said, "Let's get away from the Israelites! The* LORD *is fighting for them against Egypt." Then the* LORD *said to Moses, "Stretch out your hand over the sea so that the waters may flow back over the Egyptians and their chariots and horsemen." Moses stretched out his hand over the sea, and at daybreak the sea went back to its place. The Egyptians were fleeing toward it, and the* LORD *swept them into the sea. The water flowed back and covered the chariots and horsemen—the entire army of Pharaoh that had followed the Israelites into the sea. Not one of them survived.*   (Exodus 14:10, 13–18, 21–28)

Wow! The Israelites obeyed God's instructions and escaped what would have been certain defeat and death.

This happened shortly after the children of Israel left Egypt for the Promised Land. You would think after such an awesome display of the Lord's power—parting the sea so they could walk through it, then closing it up again so it drowned Pharaoh's army—the Israelites would be full of faith and hope. But no. Their small thinking and grumbling hearts caused the trip to take much, much longer than it should have taken. (See Numbers 14:20–35.) Finally, however, the stage was set for the crossover. Once again, the Israelites were

> LIMITED THINKING KEEPS US CONFINED IN A PROVERBIAL BOX, KILLS OUR FAITH, AND HINDERS OUR GROWTH.

challenged to think big when it was God's appointed time for them to cross the Jordan River and enter into the Promised Land.

No matter how many times we cross over to a new level with the Lord, the transition always requires big, limitless thinking. Limited thinking keeps us confined in a proverbial box, kills our faith, and hinders our growth. Limitless thinking, on the other hand, enables us to cross over, even when such a transition seems impossible in the natural realm.

Here's how it went down with the Israelites as they got ready to cross the Jordan River:

> *Joshua said to the Israelites, "Come here and listen to the words of the* LORD *your God. This is how you will know that the living God is among you and that he will certainly drive out before you the Canaanites, Hittites, Hivites, Perizzites, Girgashites, Amorites and Jebusites. See, the ark of the covenant of the Lord of all the earth will go into the Jordan ahead of you. Now then, choose twelve men from the tribes of Israel, one from each tribe. And as soon as the priests who carry the ark of the* LORD—*the Lord of all the earth*—*set foot in the Jordan, its waters flowing downstream will be cut off and stand up in a heap." So when the people broke camp to cross the Jordan, the priests carrying the ark of the covenant went ahead of them. Now the Jordan is at flood stage all during harvest. Yet as soon as the priests who carried the ark reached the Jordan and their feet touched the water's edge, the water from upstream stopped flowing. It piled up in a heap a great distance away...while the water flowing down to the [Dead] Sea...was completely cut off. So the people crossed over opposite Jericho. The priests who carried the ark of the covenant of the Lord stopped in the middle of the Jordan and stood on dry ground, while all Israel passed by until the whole nation had completed the crossing on dry ground.* (Joshua 3:9–17)

God led the children of Israel to the next level as He prepared them to take the land. It was no coincidence that they crossed the Jordan

River "*opposite Jericho.*" God had already given them the land in Jericho; they just needed to think big and cross over to possess it.

The Israelites crossed the Jordan River when it was at flood stage. Crossing the river under normal conditions took faith, but crossing when it was flooded took limitless thinking. That first step required faith, but as soon as the Israelites' feet touched the edge of the river, the power of God caused them to see big things before their very eyes. Remember, thinking big is the first step to seeing big.

The Israelites crossed over the riverbed, walking on dry ground. It wasn't muddy and there weren't any landslides. The priests "*stood on dry ground,*" as the Word tells us. You can stand firm in the midst of seemingly impossible circumstances if you think big with the mind of Christ.

OVERCOME THE SPIRIT OF LIMITATION

After the children of Israel crossed the Red Sea and escaped the bondage of Egypt, they needed to maintain their limitless thinking in order to go all the way to the Promised Land. But in the wilderness, they lost their big thinking and fell prey to the spirit of limitation. After forty years of wandering, Moses reminded them:

> *You grumbled in your tents and said, "The LORD hates us; so he brought us out of Egypt to deliver us into the hands of the Amorites to destroy us. Where can we go? Our brothers have made us lose heart. They say, 'The people are stronger and taller than we are; the cities are large, with walls up to the sky. We even saw the Anakites there.'"*　　　　　　　　　　　　　　　　(Deuteronomy 1:27–28)

The spirit of limitation launched a major attack against the Israelites. It didn't take long for it to deflate their hopes and cause them to feel defeated.

BE CAREFUL WHO YOU LISTEN TO

The children of Israel had God on their side; He orchestrated everything for their success. The only thing capable of hindering them was a mind-set of limited thinking. And when they gave in to their fears and limited think-ing—"The LORD *hates us*" and "*The people* [in the Promised Land] *are stronger and taller than we are*"—I can image the Lord was saying to Himself, as my teenage daughter likes to say, *Are you serious right now?*

The Israelites' thoughts were so far-fetched, it was ridiculous. "Really?" Moses probably wanted to say. "God brought you out of slavery only to destroy you? Does that make sense?"

> DON'T EVER LET SOMEONE ELSE'S ISSUE BECOME YOUR ISSUE.

Maybe you, too, are under a major attack by the spirit of limitation. Maybe you're in the midst of a fierce battle, whether physical, mental, emotional, or spiritual. If the enemy can convince you to limit your thinking and adopt a defeatist attitude, he can keep you from crossing over and taking all the land that he knows God has already marked for you. A strategic attack by the spirit of limitation is the enemy's only hope of preventing you from going all the way.

The Israelites told Moses, "*They say, 'The people are stronger and taller than we are...*'" (Deuteronomy 1:28). If I were Moses, I would've replied, "First off, who are *'they'* and why are you listening to them rather than to the Lord?"

We need to stop listening to what everyone else is saying to us, about us, or about our situation; instead, we need to listen to God—what He is saying today and what He has said in the past. "They" don't have any power over us or the final say—God does! "They" may be operating out of a spirit of limitation, but that doesn't mean we need to do the same.

Don't ever let someone else's issue become your issue. Shake it off and keep on living with limitless thinking. So what if the Anakites are there? Who died and left them in charge? Surely, not your big God. I don't care if all the "-ites" are there—when God has given you the land, it's a done deal. Just keep on thinking big and staying positive, and you will cross over into all the promises of God.

REMEMBER ALL THAT GOD HAS DONE FOR YOU

After reminding the Israelites about their grumbling, Moses said:

Then I said to you, "Do not be terrified; do not be afraid of them. The LORD your God, who is going before you, will fight for you, as he did for you in Egypt, before your very eyes, and in the wilderness. There you saw how the LORD your God carried you, as a father carries his son, all the way you went until you reached this place."
(Deuteronomy 1:29–31)

Moses spoke against the spirit of limitation with these words of truth, reminding the Israelites of everything the Lord had already done for them and encouraging them to believe that God would give them the victory once again.

Moses went on to say:

In spite of this, you did not trust in the LORD your God, who went ahead of you on your journey, in fire by night and in a cloud by day, to search out places for you to camp and to show you the way you should go.
(Deuteronomy 1:32)

In spite of everything the Lord had done for them and Moses's encouragement, the Israelites refused to listen. They continued to allow the spirit of limitation to dictate their future. Later, they changed their minds, deciding to go and fight the Amorites. The Lord said "no," but they went ahead anyway and were defeated. (See Deuteronomy 1:41–44).

We must get rid of the spirit of limitation before we position ourselves to fight against the enemy, or we will lose the battle. It was true for the children of Israel, and it's true for you and me today.

Do you feel continually defeated? Does it seem as if you've been losing every battle? Give your thoughts and beliefs a quick checkup.

Resist any thoughts of limitation and think big. God's got this! He knows where you are and He knows where you are going. The wilderness is not your final destination. Your promised land has already been assured to you—that's how it got its name. Your journey doesn't have to take forty years. The trip can be much quicker if you unload the spirit of limitation from your luggage and leave it behind, where it belongs.

REMEMBER, GOD DOES WHAT HE DOES "SO THAT..."

After Moses died, his assistant, Joshua, became the leader of the Israelites. Determined that they would never forget the faithfulness of God, Joshua set up a monument consisting of twelve stones taken out of the Jordan River to commemorate all that God had done on the Israelites' behalf. As he dedicated this monument, Joshua told the children of Israel:

> *In the future when your descendants ask their parents, "What do these stones mean?" tell them, "Israel crossed the Jordan on dry ground." For the* LORD *your God dried up the Jordan before you until you had crossed over. The* LORD *your God did to the Jordan what he had done to the Red Sea when he dried it up before us until we had crossed over. He did this **so that** all the peoples of the earth might know that the hand of the* LORD *is powerful and **so that** you might always fear the* LORD *your God.*   (Joshua 4:21–24)

God does things the way He does "so that" we will adopt and maintain a mind-set of limitless thinking—a mind-set like His that enables us to fulfill God-sized visions and thereby bring glory to Him. Remember, He's a big, *big* God who majors in the miraculous.

When we see "so that" in the workings of the Lord our God, it becomes easier for us to understand why He does things the way He does. God does what He does "so that" we might recognize the power of His hand at work in our lives. He does things in such a way "so that" we might always have a healthy fear of, or reverence for, Him.

God also does these things "so that" we might think like He thinks—big! Remember, nothing is impossible with the Lord. Why, then, are we so often tempted to revert to limited, small thinking? Maybe it's because the enemy is working overtime with a last-ditch effort to thwart our potential. Let's outsmart his schemes and resist the spirit of limitation and lack. Let's think big and bring God glory.

13

UNGODLY LIVING

In order for us to take all the land, we need to abide by certain standards. Even better, we need to be "standard setters" in our generation. We should refuse to go along with the crowd when it means compromising our values and violating our ethical beliefs.

The King of Kings is looking for those who will be standard setters. A standard is a model, or an example, for others to follow. A standard sets the level or measure of adequacy that establishes a goal for others to achieve.

What are our standards? And what are they communicating to those around us? If we don't set a standard, but succumb to ungodly living, God will find someone else, as He did throughout the Bible.

In the fifth chapter of Daniel, King Belshazzar of Babylon gave a great feast. He and his favored guests drank out of the gold and silver goblets that his grandfather, King Nebuchadnezzar, took from the temple in Jerusalem.

> *As they drank the wine, they praised the gods of gold and silver, of bronze, iron, wood and stone. Suddenly the fingers of a human hand appeared and wrote on the plaster of the wall, near the lampstand in the royal palace. The king watched the hand as it wrote. His face turned pale and he was so frightened that his legs became weak and his knees were knocking.* (Daniel 5:4–6)

They drank from temple goblets and praised false gods at the same time. God was not pleased.

The king needed someone to interpret the handwriting on the wall, so he *"summoned the enchanters, astrologers and diviners"* (Daniel 5:7). None of them could interpret the writing. Eventually, Daniel was summoned. (See Daniel 5:7–17.) Before reading the writing on the wall, he told the king:

> *Your Majesty, the Most High God gave your father Nebuchadnezzar sovereignty and greatness and glory and splendor....But when his heart became arrogant and hardened with pride, he was deposed from his royal throne and stripped of his glory...until he acknowledged that the Most High God is sovereign over all kingdoms on earth and sets over them anyone he wishes. But you, Belshazzar, his son, have not humbled yourself, though you knew all this. Instead, you have set yourself up against the Lord of heaven. You had the goblets from his temple brought to you, and you and your nobles, your wives and your concubines drank wine from them. You praised the gods of silver and gold, of bronze, iron, wood and stone, which cannot see or hear or understand. But you did not honor the God who holds in his hand your life and all your ways. Therefore he sent the hand that wrote the inscription.* (Daniel 5:18–23)

Daniel then translated, "*God has numbered the days of your reign and brought it to an end....You have been weighed on the scales and found wanting....Your kingdom is divided and given to the Medes and Persians*" (Daniel 5:26–28).

Belshazzar died that night. (See Daniel 5:30.)

When you occupy a position of leadership, your actions affect all of those under your influence. The King of Kings and Lord of Lords is calling for a standard of excellence in character in all areas of conduct. Just as God brought Belshazzar's reign to an end, so will He "dethrone" those who refuse to repent and set a standard of spiritual excellence by living a lifestyle of godly obedience.

If we are going to live without limits, we need the standards of the King. If not, all that we have worked so hard to attain may be lost overnight.

Yes, God is a loving and merciful God, but He is also a just God who demands a standard of conduct that is appropriate for His kingdom. He demands such a standard because He loves His people and wants the best for all His children. If we lower our standards and compromise our values, we may lose our position.

> GOD DEMANDS A STANDARD OF CONDUCT THAT IS APPROPRIATE FOR HIS KINGDOM.

CHARACTER MUST PRECEDE PROMOTION

Character is defined as "the complex of mental and ethical traits marking and often individualizing a person, group, or nation." God develops our character before He promotes us. It's an established order in His kingdom. Many times, the "commotions" and times of trial we face are actually from God's hand, intended to prepare us for upcoming promotion. It's important that we "go the steps" in the development of our character, or we may trip up in our walk with the Lord and fall down. Limitless living is all about reaching and maintaining the place of promotion that God has put us in.

Character and standards go hand in hand. Our standards are established as a result of our character, and character is the reason we abide by those standards. If we don't have outstanding character and steadfast integrity, our standards will be low and easily compromised.

I presented a teaching series several years ago that I titled "No One Takes the Elevator, Everyone Takes the Steps." In it, I talked about how everyone likes to get on an elevator, push a button, and go straight to the top. We'd like to do this in every area of our lives, not just when we're in an office building with thirty floors.

Not many people take the steps these days. Even though all of us could use the exercise, we decide we don't have time for it. We are in a rush to get where we are going, and once we get there, we rush off to the next place.

We prefer to take the elevator, no matter what the destination. We want to start in the ministry, press a button, and arrive at the top. We want our business to clip along from floor to floor, or level to level, and arrive at the top of the Fortune 500 list in no time. We want our relationships to be effortless; if we have to put any time or energy into "working through" things, we just move on to someone else.

But in the spiritual life, no one takes the elevator. Everyone is required to take the steps. These "steps" are a setup from the Lord to build Christ-like character in us.

My daughter has been a part of my ministry since she was in my womb. Over the years, I have observed in her a growing desire to be involved in various levels of leadership. I can remember when Destiny longed to be a receptionist. She thought it would be "so cool" to answer the phone all day long. If you asked her what she wanted to be when she grew up, she'd tell you that being a receptionist at Joy Ministries was her dream position. She would beg me to let her answer the phone. So, when she was about ten years old, we started to allow her to answer the switchboard after five in the evening. She was very excited and she would sit (not very patiently) and wait for the phone to ring.

It didn't take her long to realize that most phone calls to our ministry were made before five, so then she wanted to answer the phone starting at four o'clock. About a year later, we granted her request and "promoted" her.

Today, Destiny is one of the best phone counselors we have. Not only does she answer the phone, but she also runs a summer camp for children. She is taking the steps, and, as a result, she is becoming a valuable player on our ministry team.

Just as my daughter has literally grown up in the ministry, one step at a time, we all must grow up in the place and position the Lord has called us to. The growth process takes time. And it's while we are going the steps that the Lord develops our character by working *His* character into us.

SEPARATED AND CONSECRATED

The Lord invites us to think and live without limits, seizing and possessing all of the wonderful blessings He has in store for us. But only those who separate themselves from the things of the world, and consecrate themselves to the Lord, will have the power and ability to take the land.

The power of God is released in and through us as we consecrate ourselves to Him. There are a lot of people trying to live life without limits who fail because they are neither separated nor consecrated. They look like the world, they talk like the world, they act like the world, and, sometimes, they even smell like the world.

Separation from the world is the first step toward consecration to God. Without holiness, limitless thinking and limitless living simply aren't possible. It may seem as if things are working for a little while, but then, when we least expect it, everything will come tumbling down around us. Our foundation must be built to last through every storm, and the only foundation that promises such stability is a holy lifestyle.

We cannot live a holy life if we aren't separated from the things of the world and consecrated to the things of God.

My favorite definition of the verb *separate* comes from *Webster's New World College Dictionary*: "to single out or set apart from others for a special purpose." We must separate ourselves from the things of the world so we can consecrate ourselves to the things of God.

Once again, separation must precede consecration. Ask yourself: *Is it easy to distinguish my life from the lives of others around me? Can people tell that my life is different because of my commitment to God, or do I blend in with the crowd?* When we are separated, people notice. And when God has singled us out and set us apart from others, it's because of His special purpose for our lives.

I haven't lived like "everyone else" since the time I was saved, at age seventeen. Even other believers do things that the Holy Spirit doesn't allow me to do. I don't judge such people; I don't whine and complain about the fact that I'm not supposed to do certain things. I only know what the Lord has said to me, year after year, time after time: *"Much is required from those to whom much is given"* (Luke 12:48 TLB). Yes, the Lord has given me much, so I'm often required to pay a higher price than others for separation and consecration. But it's always well worth it.

Maybe today, you are counting the cost. Let me tell you, the price you pay for living a holy, separated life is always worth it. When you are separated, you can be consecrated. And when you are consecrated, you experience the power, the presence, and the glory of God in a way beyond compare.

PURE, NOT MIXED

I like to cook, but I like baking even more—probably because I love eating the baked goods that come out of my oven. One thing I've learned from baking is the right combination, or mixture, is absolutely scrumptious, while the wrong mixture of ingredients is disgusting.

Children often like to play kitchen and mix random ingredients together to make a "special concoction." Destiny loved playing this game, whether we were eating at home or dining in a restaurant. She would add "secret" ingredients when no one was looking, such as excessive amounts of salt, ketchup, or other things that had no business being mixed into other items. The brave soul who dared to sample her creations would be sick to the stomach for several hours afterward. Whenever Destiny managed to talk me into sampling her "secret recipe," I usually started gagging and would spit it right out of my mouth. It was a reaction over which I had no control.

Using the "mixture game," I taught Destiny the danger of mixture in the Christian life. The proper combination of the right ingredients is awesome, but a mixture of wrong ingredients makes us sick.

The effect of spiritual mixture in our lives is the same. It causes God to spit us out, so to speak. He reproved the church in Laodicea with the following words:

> I know your deeds, that you are neither cold nor hot. I wish you were either one or the other! So, because you are lukewarm—neither hot nor cold—I am about to spit you out of my mouth.
>
> (Revelation 3:15–16)

Some Christians concoct their own "secret mixtures" of habits and practices as they endeavor to live their lives for the Lord. The book of Revelation tells us the Lord wants us to be on fire for Him. We are to be hot and fiery Christians, not lukewarm, wishy-washy believers who lead lives of carnal desires mixed with Christian disciplines, or pious behavior mixed with compromise and "minor sins." That kind of mixture in our spiritual lives makes the Lord grieved and heartsick.

Mix is defined as "to combine or blend into one mass; to bring into close association." Be very careful about who and what you are "mixing" and joining together with. When you mix together with

WE SHOULD BE HOT AND FIERY CHRISTIANS, NOT LUKEWARM, WISHY-WASHY BELIEVERS.

someone or something, you are bound to that person, spirit, habit, or way of life. Don't unite yourself with anyone or anything grievous to the Holy Spirit. We believers are supposed to be light in the midst of darkness. (See Ephesians 5:8.) We'd better make sure the darkness is not putting out our light.

When we have slipped and fallen into ungodliness, let us remember this charge in Acts 3:19: *"Repent, then, and turn to God, so that your sins may be wiped out, that times of refreshing may come from the Lord."*

Sin separates us from the presence of the Lord. We can't live a lifestyle of compromise and expect the glorious presence of the Lord to surround us. Living a lifestyle of holiness opens the door for the refreshing presence of the Lord to be our portion. There's nothing more refreshing to our spirit, soul, or body than to live in the presence of the Lord.

CONSECRATION IS A PERSONAL PROCESS

Consecrating ourselves to the Lord involves making right choices and righteous decisions. No one else can do it for us. We must do it ourselves, relying on the power and strength of the Holy Spirit to help us.

Webster's New World College Dictionary defines *consecrate* as "to set apart as holy; make or declare sacred…; to devote entirely; dedicate." God has appointed us and called us to be set apart as His own. We must stop joining ourselves with people, places, and things that are opposed to the consecration God has ordained for our lives. God has called us to be set apart; now, we have to consecrate ourselves daily to the Lord and the things of God.

Let's not undo all that the Lord has done in our lives by getting "stuck on stupid." Every day, people make impulsive choices and foolish decisions that cost them their anointing. Don't be one of those people! There's too much at stake. God has planned a long list of wonderful feats for you to make, and lands for you to take, that will glorify Him and build His kingdom. Pay the price for holiness by living separated and consecrated. You will always be glad you did.

Joshua instructed the Israelites he was leading, *"Consecrate your-selves, for tomorrow the* LORD *will do amazing things among you"* (Joshua 3:5). Tomorrow—and even today—the Lord wants to do amazing things in you, through you, and for you. But it will require you to live a life of consecration unto the Lord.

Without consecration, your potential is limited. God's desire is for there to be no limits on the amazing, miraculous, and supernatural things that you do for Him and His kingdom. But unless you're living a holy, separated life of consecration to Him, limits in those areas are inevitable.

I have confidence that you will do what it takes to live a life of separation and consecration to God, so amazing, miraculous things will begin to unfold in and through your life. A life without limits is your portion, my friend!

14

UNWHOLESOME SPEECH

Have you ever noticed that people in the world speak very freely, seeming not to care what comes out of their mouths? They curse loudly, criticize liberally, and joke crudely.

They fail to realize that when we obey the Lord with our speech, we're actually worshipping Him. Yes, our obedience is worship, because all acts of obedience to the Lord count as worship. And there are always blessings waiting on the other side of obedience.

In God's eyes, obedience in the first place is preferable to the sacrifices necessary to atone for disobedience. As we read in the first book of Samuel:

> *Does the* LORD *delight in burnt offerings and sacrifices as much as in obeying the* LORD? *To obey is better than sacrifice, and to heed is better than the fat of rams.* (1 Samuel 15:22)

As we obey the Lord in our speech, we set ourselves up to receive great blessings from Him. Psalm 128:1 says, *"Blessed are all who fear the* LORD, *who walk in obedience to him."* Our job is to speak the Word, pray the Word, and declare the Word. God's Word never returns to Him empty or void.

> *As the rain and the snow come down from heaven, and do not return to it without watering the earth and making it bud and flourish, so that it yields seed for the sower and bread for the eater, so is my word that goes out from my mouth: It will not return to me empty, but will accomplish what I desire and achieve the purpose for which I sent it.* (Isaiah 55:10–11)

God's Word always produces fruit. That's why the enemy doesn't want us to spend time in the Word. We must get back to basics and keep the Word as our foundation—keep speaking the Word to people, keep praying the Word over people and situations, and keep declaring the Word over our own circumstances.

OPEN YOUR MOUTH AND DEFEAT THE GIANT

You will never defeat a giant with your mouth shut. You have been given all authority in the name of Jesus, as He told His disciples. (See Luke 10:19.) What are you doing with your authority? When you speak the name of Jesus and invoke the authority you have been given in His name, there's no giant you can't defeat.

We see a literal example of this truth in the story of David and Goliath, which we discussed in chapter eleven. David knew the power he had in God's name and he wasn't afraid to use it.

SPEAK VICTORY ALONE

David defeated the giant Goliath first and foremost with his words. Too often, we defeat ourselves with the words we speak from our own mouths. But when we expect big things, our words line up with the expectation in our hearts.

David told Goliath he was going to fight him "*in the name of the* Lord *Almighty, the God of the armies of Israel, whom you have defied. This day the* Lord *will deliver you into my hands, and I'll strike you down and cut off your head*" (1 Samuel 17:45–46).

David was "*little more than a boy, glowing with health and handsome, and* [Goliath] *despised him*" (1 Samuel 17:42). But David declared the Word! He was calling things that were not as though they were, just as God does. (See Romans 4:17 kjv.) And David anticipated immediate and decisive victory, "*this very day.*"

Are you expecting a long, drawn-out battle with an uncertain outcome? Or are you expecting nothing less than total, immediate victory? Our battles may sometimes last a little longer than we would prefer, but in some cases, that may be because of what comes out of our mouths. We shouldn't speak anything less than total victory.

David opened his mouth and declared victory before his showdown with Goliath even began. That's why the battle was so brief. David declared victory with his mouth, as proof of his heart of expectation, and the giant who had intimated everyone else came down with one hit from David's slingshot. All David had at his disposal were five stones, but only one was needed to bring down the giant.

What are you expecting today? Are you expecting big? When you expect big, your giants are defeated, first with your mouth as you declare victory against them, then with a small, simple stone that's backed by an army of angelic forces.

The "big boys," including Goliath, laughed at young David. But the truth is, they were intimidated by the faith-filled declarations that demonstrated David's level of expectation. Allow your expectation level to intimidate the enemy today, and open your mouth to defeat every giant that comes against you.

CLAIM YOUR AUTHORITY IN JESUS'S NAME

As David spoke the Word, angels were activated to assist him. He later wrote:

Praise the LORD, you his angels, you mighty ones who do his bidding, who obey his word. (Psalm 103:20)

When we expect and declare victory with our mouths, angelic forces are released on our behalf.

It wasn't the stone that took down Goliath; it was the host of angelic forces behind the stone, which was launched in faith out of a heart of expectation.

God is waiting for you to raise your expectation and speak accordingly, invoking your divine authority to release angels on your behalf. Are you expecting angelic forces to win the battle for you? Or are you still trying to weigh whether you have enough faith to launch an attack?

> GOD IS WAITING FOR YOU TO RAISE YOUR EXPECTATION AND SPEAK ACCORDINGLY.

You don't need the CIA working with you. You don't need a SWAT team. You have God's angels—the mighty ones who obey His Word—ready to work on your behalf. Keep declaring the Word out loud. When you do, the angels hear it and go to work for you. I know who I want on my team. Do you? Then speak accordingly.

No matter what schemes or tactics the enemy uses against you, when you approach the situation armed with the authority that is yours in the name of Jesus, you will always win. Remember, you and God together are the majority, no matter the odds stacked against you—and God's team always wins. Keep declaring the Word, and victory will be yours, in Jesus's name.

REFUSE TO SPEAK DEFEAT

Sometimes, the overwhelming circumstances of life gradually lower our level of expectation. Consider the widow in Zarephath in chapter seventeen of the first book of Kings. By the time she crossed paths with the prophet Elijah, her expectation level was nil. When Elijah asked her for some water and bread, she replied:

> As surely as the LORD your God lives…I don't have any bread— only a handful of flour in a jar and a little olive oil in a jug. I am gathering a few sticks to take home and make a meal for myself and my son, that we may eat it—and die.　　(1 Kings 17:12)

The only thing the widow expected was imminent death. Her thoughts and words reflected a mind-set of total defeat. A spirit of fear dampened her expectation to its lowest possible level. But her heavenly Father, out of His love for her, sent to her a man of God who was full of faith and expectation.

> Elijah said to her, "Don't be afraid. Go home and do as you have said. But first make a small loaf of bread for me from what you have and bring it to me, and then make something for yourself and your son. For this is what the LORD, the God of Israel, says: 'The jar of flour will not be used up and the jug of oil will not run dry until the day the LORD sends rain on the land.'"　　(1 Kings 17:13–14)

Elijah's sense of expectation and words of assurance ushered the widow and her son into a place of supernatural turnaround. Sure enough, here's what happened when they followed his instructions:

> There was food every day for Elijah and for the woman and her family. For the jar of flour was not used up and the jug of oil did not run dry, in keeping with the word of the LORD spoken by Elijah.
> 　　　　　　　　　　　　　　　　　　(1 Kings 17:15–16)

The prophet's expectation not only changed the situation, it changed lives. Your own sense of expectation, spoken aloud, has the power to release the supernatural in the lives of those around you.

It seems the woman hadn't fully learned her lesson, however. Later, her son got sick and nearly died. Did she speak in faith, declaring his healing? No, she turned to Elijah with these words of accusation: *"What do you have against me...? Did you come to remind me of my sin and kill my son?"* (1 Kings 17:18).

Once again, Elijah's words of faith saved the day. Positioning himself over the nearly lifeless body of the widow's son, he prayed, *"LORD my God, let this boy's life return to him!"* (1 Kings 17:21).

God heard Elijah's cry and restored life to the widow's son. (See 1 Kings 17:22.) Finally, the truth dawned on the widow. She declared to Elijah, *"Now I know that you are a man of God and that the word of the LORD from your mouth is the truth"* (1 Kings 17:24).

Before the prophet Elijah showed up, the widow was declaring certain defeat. Thoughts of victory were nowhere to be found in her thinking, her expectations, or her speech.

When you expect big things, you count on victory. And when you count on victory, you declare victory, not defeat, even before the battle begins.

For those who don't maintain high expectations, this kind of thinking seems impractical or even ludicrous. When David volunteered to take on the giant, most people thought he was being impractical, ludicrous, and just plain crazy. But David expected victory, and victory is what God gave him when he spoke victory in faith.

Just as the widow's mouth revealed that she expected defeat, David's mouth manifested his expectation of victory. David never even considered defeat as an option; it never crossed his mind. He was 100 percent confident that he would prevail over the enemy, and he spoke accordingly.

SURRENDER YOUR TONGUE

The Word says, *"If you are willing and obedient, you will eat the good things of the land"* (Isaiah 1:19). In order for you and me to go all the way, possess all the promises of God, and eat the "good things," we must be willing and obedient to daily surrender all, including our tongues—the words we speak from our mouths.

The Bible is full of warnings about unwholesome speech. The words we speak are an overflow of what is in our hearts. Jesus said, *"The mouth speaks what the heart is full of"* (Matthew 12:34; Luke 6:45). James has a particularly strong statement on this topic, saying an untamed tongue *"corrupts the whole body, sets the whole course of one's life on fire, and is itself set on fire by hell"* (James 3:6). Sobering, isn't it?

We find a more positive message from the book of Ephesians:

> *Do not let any unwholesome talk come out of your mouths, but only what is helpful for building others up according to their needs, that it may benefit those who listen. And do not grieve the Holy Spirit of God, with whom you were sealed for the day of redemption. Get rid of all bitterness, rage and anger, brawling and slander, along with every form of malice. Be kind and compassionate to one another, forgiving each other, just as in Christ God forgave you.*
>
> (Ephesians 4:29–32)

This passage starts with the phrase *"Do not let…."* The implication is that we have a choice. We must choose not to "let" unwholesome talk leave our mouths. The tongue is the most accurate reflection of the heart. If we harbor unforgiveness or bitterness in our hearts, our tongues will expose the evidence of that quicker than anything else.

When someone verbally attacks you, that person's words don't define who you are, but rather reveal the nature of his or her character.

THE WORDS THAT COME OUT OF OUR MOUTHS EXPOSE THE CONDITION OF OUR HEARTS.

The same is true for you and me: the words that come out of our mouths expose the condition of our hearts. When we "let" ourselves utter unwholesome talk, it grieves the

Holy Spirit. We must be careful not to grieve the Holy Spirit in any area of our lives, by what we say, what we do, what we think, or what we allow ourselves to be exposed to.

Whenever we are about to speak, we should pause to weigh our words, asking ourselves such questions as:

- *Is what I'm about to say helpful in building up my listeners?*

- *Is it going to benefit those people in their hearts and in their spiritual conditions before the Lord?*

- *Will the Holy Spirit be grieved by what's about to come out of my mouth?*

Before we say anything, we should examine the condition of our own hearts and the motivation behind our speech. There may be a few things we need to surrender to the Lord and repent of first. Jesus said:

> *Everyone will have to give account on the day of judgment for every empty word they have spoken. For by your words you will be acquitted, and by your words you will be condemned.*
> (Matthew 12:36–37)

I don't want any careless, empty words coming out of my mouth. Do you?

DON'T GIVE VOICE TO DOUBT AND NEGATIVITY

Some people grumble at the tiniest sign of opposition, not realizing that, in most cases, opposition presents an opportunity for promotion. The key is our focus. When we focus on the "fight," or on all of the things that are going wrong or could go wrong, the enemy is likely to deceive us into feeling all alone and overpowered. But when we focus on the fruit that the Lord wants to produce in and through us, we remember that all the power of heaven is on our side.

We are anything but overpowered. The only power Satan has is the amount he manages to talk us into believing he has. Don't allow your own words to be your downfall! Don't be discouraged or defeated by your own faulty beliefs or negative self-talk. Declare God's promises with your mouth and make sure those are the "overflow" of your heart.

PAY ATTENTION TO WHAT YOU SAY ABOUT GOD

You can learn a lot about a person just by listening to him speak. We need to pay attention to the words that come out of our mouths, especially when the topic of conversation is our God. The psalmist writes, "*I will say of the LORD, 'He is my refuge and my fortress, my God, in whom I trust'*" (Psalm 91:2).

What have we been saying of the Lord? Have we been saying, "Lord, this isn't fair"? "Lord, You must not love me because of all the hardships I'm facing"? In the midst of life's storms and trials, we need to say, "Lord, You are my refuge. Lord, You are my fortress. God, I trust You. I lean on You. I am confident in Your ability to bring me through this difficult season."

As we dwell in the secret place of the Most High and tell the Lord that He is our refuge and our fortress, we set ourselves up for success in the midst of any storm or scheme of the enemy that comes our way.

Another translation puts it this way: "*I will say of the Lord, He is my Refuge and my Fortress, my God; on Him I lean and rely, and in Him I* [confidently] *trust!*" (Psalm 91:2 AMPC).

Again, it's crucial to be aware of we are saying of the Lord. The Word tells us that we should be calling Him our refuge and our fortress, proclaiming our unfailing trust in Him.

Yet, oftentimes, we say just the opposite. Sometimes, we say, "This isn't fair. Why is God forcing me to go through all this? Why do I always have it so hard, while everyone else has it so easy?" When we speak such doubt-filled statements, it reflects a faulty understanding of God and His benefits, which are available to all His children.

The Word says, *"The steps of a man are established by the* LORD*"* (Psalm 37:23 NASB). God has ordered our steps, so if we are complaining, then we are speaking negatively about something that God has allowed.

God is in control of everything. He hasn't fallen off His throne just because we're in the middle of a crisis, facing a giant, or dealing with a problem. As we say the right things about the Lord and speak rightly of the steps He has ordered on our behalf, we can maintain a godly perspective, no matter our circumstances. From this perspective, we're empowered and fueled by faith to take all the land that God has for us.

15

FOLLOWING THE CROWD

Many people have become deceived regarding the truth. As Jesus told His disciples:

> *This people's heart has become calloused; they hardly hear with their ears, and they have closed their eyes. Otherwise they might see with their eyes, hear with their ears, understand with their hearts and turn, and I would heal them.* (Matthew 13:15)

I want to encourage you to stand continually on the Word of truth. It doesn't matter what everyone else is doing; it matters only what the Word of God—His written Word (the Bible), as well as His *rhema* (revealed) words, which always align with His written Word—tells us to do. If there is a contradiction between something you perceive to be a revelation from God and what the Bible teaches, you must question the validity of the "revealed word" you claim to have received.

TAKE A STAND FOR RIGHTEOUSNESS

> IT DOESN'T MATTER WHAT EVERYONE ELSE IS DOING; IT MATTERS ONLY WHAT THE WORD OF GOD TELLS US TO DO.

God's Word is the ultimate truth. Yet many people's hearts have become calloused to the truth, and more will follow in these last days. Many people are deaf and blind to what the Lord is saying and doing. *"But as for me and my house, we will serve the* LORD*"* (Joshua 24:15 NASB).

How about you? Are you willing to stand for righteousness, no matter what it may cost? You have to be willing to stand on the Word of God, even when you *feel* alone and isolated. I say "feel" because you are never actually alone in your stand for righteousness. The Lord is with you always, even until the end of the world. (See Matthew 28:20.)

When folks want to argue with you about matters of doctrine or truth, don't argue; just stand. Stand on the Word of truth, and when you have done all, keep standing. (See Ephesians 6:13.) I never allow myself to get pulled into arguments or debates about the Word of truth. I simply share what the Lord has done for me because no one can argue with a personal testimony. I just say that I agree with what the Word says about the issue at hand. The Word is the ultimate truth and that is my stance on every issue.

It isn't always easy taking a stand for righteousness. The righteous stance can be a very lonely place. But even there, we are not alone, because the One who is righteousness embodied stands with us. He also makes note of who stands with Him and who opposes Him, and He will reward or punish both groups accordingly.

Take a look at some remarks Jesus made on this very matter:

The Son of Man will send out his angels, and they will weed out of his kingdom everything that causes sin and all who do evil. They will throw them into the blazing furnace, where there will be weeping and gnashing of teeth. Then the righteous will shine like the sun in the kingdom of their Father. Whoever has ears, let them hear.
(Matthew 13:41–43)

Thank goodness it isn't up to us to penalize those who aren't standing for righteousness. God will take care of the "weeds." It's not our job to be "weed-wackers" in the kingdom. We just need to remain focused on having ears to hear what the Spirit of the Lord is saying, for that's where our time and energy belong.

Even as we patiently wait for the day of reckoning, we must remember that we are not alone in our stand for righteousness. The Lord wants us to hear His voice as He stands with us, right by our side. Not only is the Lord with us, but we are surrounded by a heavenly host of angels ready to fight on our behalf.

AVOID OFFENDING AND TAKING OFFENSE

It can also be lonely when we feel offended, belittled, and rejected by our peers as we stand on the truth instead of following the crowd. Take heart and remember that Jesus knows just how you feel. Check out some of the things He told His disciples along these lines:

You will be hated by everyone because of me, but the one who stands firm to the end will be saved. (Matthew 10:22)

If the world hates you, keep in mind that it hated me first. If you belonged to the world, it would love you as its own. As it is, you do not belong to the world, but I have chosen you out of the world. That is why the world hates you. (John 15:18–19)

In all my talk about embracing solitude—since we are never really alone when we know God as our Savior—I don't want to undercut the importance of living in a committed Christian community. We believers need one another to bolster our faith, shoulder our burdens, and boost our spirits. Thus, while within our family of fellow believers, we must strive to promote harmony and resolve disagreements quickly.

This is especially true of our conduct as we seek to win souls for the kingdom of God. A big part of this is being slow to take offense. *"Whoever would foster love covers over an offense, but whoever repeats the matter separates close friends"* (Proverbs 17:9). Whenever someone does or says something that ruffles our feathers, we should seek to promote love by forgiving our offender and moving on, rather than promoting discord and disunity by repeating the matter to someone else or mentally rehashing the offense.

Living this out requires major self-restraint. Our flesh would rather talk about the offense and seek comfort from others who would side with us. The best thing to do when we've been offended is to keep our mouths shut and our hearts right. If we talk about the offense or the offender with anyone other than our heavenly Father, we may cause division among other people, while also stirring up unforgiveness and bitterness in our own hearts.

The sooner we release an offense by covering over it—keeping our mouths shut and our hearts right—the more effectively we can promote love. God is love and His heart is always for us to walk in and promote love, no matter the circumstances.

Proverbs 19:11 says, *"A person's wisdom yields patience; it is to one's glory to overlook an offense."* It also takes great patience to overlook an offense. Our flesh just wants to jump in there and retaliate against our offenders as payback for the pain they have caused us. But wisdom tells us to be patient with those people as they grow in character and progress in their walk with the Lord.

A decision to overlook an offense brings glory to our heavenly Father, while a choice to repeat the matter, to rehash and dwell on our pain, is counterproductive, not to mention a hindrance to love.

FOLLOWING THE CROWD 193

The best thing we can do is release each offense immediately to the Lord by forgiving whoever has hurt us. As I like to say, "Don't nurse it, don't rehearse it—just curse it at the root." When we nurse a hurt, we wallow in self-pity and sit around moping. When we "rehearse" it, we may tell anyone who will listen about how poorly we were treated, or we may review the offense time and time again in our minds.

Nursing and rehearsing a hurt are not healthy ways of dealing with offenses. We must curse every offense at the root so bitterness and unforgiveness are not given an opportunity to grow in our hearts. We curse an offense by praying for those who have hurt and offended us, and by allowing the Holy Spirit to minister healing to our hearts. We also curse an offense by declaring the Word of God over ourselves and our situation, and refusing to bemoan how unfairly we were treated.

JESUS, THE MASTER OF FORGIVENESS

Jesus modeled perfectly how we should handle offenses. His reaction was simple: he shook them off. He turned the other cheek. He stayed focused on His Father's business, and He didn't let anything or anyone shake Him.

> Coming to his hometown, [Jesus] began teaching the people in their synagogue, and they were amazed. "Where did this man get this wisdom and these miraculous powers?" they asked. "Isn't this the carpenter's son? Isn't his mother's name Mary, and aren't his brothers James, Joseph, Simon and Judas? Aren't all his sisters with us? Where then did this man get all these things?" And they took offense at him. But Jesus said to them, "A prophet is not without honor except in his own town and in his own home."
>
> (Matthew 13:54–57)

The people took offense at Jesus, even though He was doing exactly what the Father had sent Him to do, at the exact time and in the exact place His Father had sent Him to do it. If you know that you are in the right place at the right time, doing the right thing, with the right heart motive, nothing should shake you—not even the indignation of the "religious folk" around you.

> IF YOUR PRINCIPLES, VALUES, AND RIGHTEOUS LIFESTYLE CAUSE OFFENSE AMONG OTHER PEOPLE, YOU ARE IN GOOD COMPANY.

Just be the person God has called you to be. Stand on the Word of God. If other people are offended, don't let their issue become your issue. Jesus wasn't offended by the offense that others took at Him. He just stood His ground, shook the dust from His feet, and kept on keeping on!

If your principles, values, and righteous lifestyle cause offense among other people, you are in good company. That's exactly what happened to Jesus Christ, the King of Kings and Lord of Lords. And never forget about the heavenly host of angels that surround you.

STAND WITH FELLOW BELIEVERS

My favorite example of a group of regular people taking a stand for righteousness is found in the third chapter of the book of Daniel. It's the story of Shadrach, Meshach, and Abednego—three brave, godly men who prized their commitment to the Lord above their very lives.

King Nebuchadnezzar had arranged for the construction of a gold idol he wanted everyone to bow before and worship. All of his subjects obeyed except for these three men, who had been appointed by the king as administrators over Babylon. (See Daniel 2:49.) The king summoned them and said:

> *"Is it true, Shadrach, Meshach and Abednego, that you do not serve my gods or worship the image of gold I have set up? Now when you hear the sound of the horn, flute, zither, lyre, harp, pipe and all kinds of music, if you are ready to fall down and worship the image I made, very good. But if you do not worship it, you will be thrown immediately into a blazing furnace. Then what god will be able to rescue you*

from my hand?" Shadrach, Meshach and Abednego replied to him, "King Nebuchadnezzar, we do not need to defend ourselves before you in this matter. If we are thrown into the blazing furnace, the God we serve is able to save us from it, and he will deliver us from Your Majesty's hand. But even if he does not, we want you to know, Your Majesty, that we will not serve your gods or worship the image of gold you have set up." (Daniel 3:14–18)

You know you're taking a stand for righteousness when you stop trying to defend yourself and simply trust in the Lord, come what may. God is always able to deliver you, but even if He doesn't, will you still stand for righteousness?

I believe we need to decide right now that we will always stand for the Lord and for His righteousness, even if doing so costs us our lives. It sounds extreme, but if someone put a gun to your face, would you deny the Lord? Or would you boldly state your allegiance to God? You are never alone in your stand, but you must decide now that you will never bow down to anything less than the King of Kings and Lord of Lords.

Then Nebuchadnezzar was furious with Shadrach, Meshach and Abednego, and his attitude toward them changed. He ordered the furnace heated seven times hotter than usual and commanded some of the strongest soldiers in his army to tie [them] up...and throw them into the blazing furnace. (Daniel 3:19–20)

Folks may change their attitude toward you overnight. Even so, just keep on standing for righteousness. People may heat up their attacks against you; if so, just stand. They may make things seven or even seventy times worse. Just stand. They may throw you into the pit or toss you in a fiery furnace. Keep standing for righteousness and standing up on the truth. You are not alone!

Shadrach, Meshach, and Abednego stood together. They were in it to win it. They stood side by side. Oh, that we believers in these last days would stand together! We need each other more now than ever before. We need to stop arguing and backbiting; we must stand side by side against the idols, deceptions, and other evils so prevalent in our world today.

> *Then King Nebuchadnezzar leaped to his feet in amazement and asked his advisers, "Weren't there three men that we tied up and threw into the fire?" They replied, "Certainly, Your Majesty." He said, "Look! I see four men walking around in the fire, unbound and unharmed, and the fourth looks like a son of the gods."*
>
> (Daniel 3:24–25)

Not only did these three exceptional men stand together, but there was a fourth man in the fire with them. Perhaps it was the pre-incarnate Jesus or an angel. No matter who it was, the Lord is always right there with us, empowering us by His Holy Spirit to keep standing in the midst of opposition, spiritual warfare, and fiery trials.

Nebuchadnezzar went to the opening of the furnace and shouted, *"Shadrach, Meshach and Abednego, servants of the Most High God, come out! Come here!"* (Daniel 3:26). So the three came out and *"the fire had not harmed their bodies, nor was a hair of their heads singed; their robes were not scorched, and there was no smell of fire on them"* (Daniel 3:27).

When God delivers you, He delivers you all the way. They didn't even smell like smoke. Now, do you think they were alone in that furnace? Not for a minute! And neither are you. Don't listen to the enemy's lies and believe anything different. You are not alone in your stand for righteousness and holy living, for God stands on your side; He will deliver you, in one way or another.

> *Then Nebuchadnezzar said, "Praise be to the God of Shadrach, Meshach and Abednego, who has sent his angel and rescued his servants! They trusted in him and defied the king's command and were willing to give up their lives rather than serve or worship any god except their own God. Therefore I decree that the people of any nation or language who say anything against the God of Shadrach, Meshach and Abednego be cut into pieces and their houses be turned*

into piles of rubble, for no other god can save in this way."
(Daniel 3:28–29)

The stand of Shadrach, Meshach, and Abednego brought about a total turnaround in the kingdom. God didn't just deliver the three Hebrew children; He totally transformed the king and the nation that he ruled, for His glory. Your stand in these last days will usher in a total turnaround in the lives of those around you.

King Nebuchadnezzar experienced a total turnaround, and then he led the nation to the same place of turnaround. That's powerful and prophetic. As you and I take a stand for righteousness and refuse to bow down to idols or practice immoral behavior, our choices will usher in a needed turnaround in the lives of others. The world is looking for folks who will stand up for the truth.

The third chapter of Daniel concludes, *"Then the king promoted Shadrach, Meshach and Abednego in the province of Babylon"* (Daniel 3:30). Promotion always follows the trial when you have passed through it faithfully. Will you pass the test and be blessed with promotion?

As we close this chapter, let me leave you with the following charge from Joshua 1:9: *"Have I not commanded you? Be strong and courageous. Do not be afraid; do not be discouraged, for the LORD your God will be with you wherever you go."*

Limitless thinking and limitless living present a continual challenge for us to be strong and courageous as we lead holy lives. As we remember daily that we are not alone in our stand for righteousness, because the Lord is with us, it keeps our focus on the finish line of victory. God truly is with us wherever we go, in every pit and fiery furnace.

16

IMPATIENCE

Proverbs 13:12 says, *"Hope deferred makes the heart sick, but a longing fulfilled is a tree of life."* I think we have all experienced "deferred hope," waiting for what felt like an eternity for something we desired to come to pass.

Many of the good things we want will require a long wait. But when our ultimate hope is in the right place—not in an earthly desire, but in the divine Person of God Himself, who will never fail us—we can be content even while we're waiting for His promises to be fulfilled in our lives.

Hope is a vital part of limitless thinking and limitless living. That's why we've got to be sure our hope is in the proper place. Hope may be deferred in a certain area of your life, but that doesn't mean hope has been denied. Don't get stuck in the "heartsick" state if a hope of yours has been deferred for the time being. Just keep your hope in the Lord. He's the God of hope.

> IF OUR HOPE IS IN ANYONE OR ANYTHING BESIDES THE LORD, WE WILL BE CRESTFALLEN.

I love this verse from the book of Romans: *"May the God of hope fill you with all joy and peace as you trust in him, so that you may overflow with hope by the power of the Holy Spirit"* (Romans 15:13). God is not only the source of all hope, He *is* hope! When our hope is in God, we can be filled with all joy and peace, no matter what's going on around us. When our hope is in the Lord, we are continually filled with God-inspired expectation.

But if our hope is in anyone or anything besides the Lord, we will be crestfallen, our expectations left unfulfilled. One sure way to be disappointed and discouraged is to place unrealistic expectations on other people or events to make us happy and fulfilled. Other people will let us down; they are only human, just like you and me. But when our hope is in the Lord, we can overflow with hope that also buoys the expectation level of those around us.

I can't emphasize it enough: our hope should never be in other people, our paycheck, or our circumstances. Our hope should always be in the Lord. When our hope is in the right place, our expectations have a solid foundation and are bound to be fulfilled. In the meantime, we ourselves will be filled with the presence of the Lord, which satisfies like nothing else.

TRUST PATIENTLY IN GOD'S TIMING

Sometimes, we are raring to go and conquer the land, only to hear Father God say to us, "Now's not the time." And then, when we've reached the point of nearly losing sight of the vision, He says, "Okay, now's the time." Usually, when His time arrives, we are so dead to the vision that we want to stay parked on the couch. The last thing we feel like doing is getting up and taking the land. But when the time fully comes, God calls us forth to conquer new territory.

Father God is asking many of us today, as Joshua asked the Israelites, *"How long will you wait before you begin to take possession of the land that the Lord, the God of your ancestors, has given you?"* (Joshua 18:3). We just need to *begin* when He says to. We may think it isn't the right time, but in many cases, that's our first confirmation that it is God's appointed time.

In our natural mind, we may generate a hundred reasons why now couldn't possibly be the right time. But the perfect time is when we aren't fueled by selfish motivations, such as a search for fame or glory. When it's God's timing, we have to depend 100 percent on the Lord. God has chosen now because we have died to the vision. We have died to our flesh and can't rely on anything in the natural—our strength, our ingenuity, our charisma, or our resources. When it's the divinely appointed time, the stage is set for God to get all the glory. We, and everyone around us, will know without a doubt that it was God, and God alone, who gave us this land.

One key to keeping expectation alive is realizing that we rarely understand God's timing. It's not our place to determine the proper time for something to occur or a promise to be fulfilled. It's our job to keep expectation alive in our hearts so we can keep expecting big things from the supernatural hand of God. God moves at the speed of supernatural, but always according to His timing, not ours.

When God's will and God's time intersect, the promises of God are suddenly fulfilled. It will never happen a day early or a day late. God is always right on time. Just when we are about to throw in the towel, after we have died a thousand deaths to the vision, God will move supernaturally, if we just keep on expecting.

We waste so much time trying to figure things out on our own. We waste so much energy trying to give God a hand and speed things up.

He doesn't need our help; He only needs our obedience. When we are obedient to keep expectation alive in our hearts and wait patiently on Him, He will move in instant, when we least expect it.

The psalmist said, *"I wait for the LORD, my whole being waits, and in his word I put my hope"* (Psalm 130:5). This verse exhorts us to put our hope in the word of the Lord—both His written Word and the *rhema* or revealed words He speaks to us, either directly or through one of His prophets. Don't lose hope while you wait. Keep expectation alive in your heart.

FIND ENCOURAGEMENT IN GOD'S WORD

Joshua received a word from the Lord that really fueled his expectation:

> The LORD said to Joshua, *"Do not be afraid; do not be discouraged. Take the whole army with you, and go up and attack Ai. For I have delivered into your hands the king of Ai, his people, his city and his land. You shall do to Ai and its king as you did to Jericho and its king, except that you may carry off their plunder and livestock for yourselves. Set an ambush behind the city."*
>
> (Joshua 8:1–2)

When God says it, that settles it! All you have to do is keep expectation alive in your heart and you will see God fulfill all of His promises in His timing. Get in the presence of the Lord today, listen for a word from Him, and then stand on the Word as you wait for the fulfillment of His promise.

Too many people lose their sense of expectation or give up hope when they don't hear from the Lord immediately in response to a prayer, or when they've heard from Him, but don't immediately see His word coming to pass. Just keep hope and expectation alive in your heart. Before you know it, God will move at the speed of supernatural on your behalf.

RESIST THE TEMPTATION TO "HELP" GOD OUT

For most of us, waiting patiently on God's timing presents a serious challenge. We don't mind keeping our sense of expectation alive for a day or two. We can even go a few weeks, if we absolutely must. But after that, we get tired of waiting. The life span of our expectation level doesn't usually exceed thirty days.

That was the problem with Abraham and Sarah. Their expectation died prematurely, so they came up with a "great plan" that didn't turn out so great. They decided to "help" God out.

Have you ever tried to give God a hand, only to find yourself in a bigger mess than when you started? We talked earlier about how Abraham and Sarah wanted to expedite the fulfillment of God's promise to them—the promise of a son and eventual offspring who would outnumber the stars in the sky. (See Genesis 15:4–5.) As they waited, their sense of expectation dwindled; due to their "intervention," the size of their mess grew. (See Genesis 16.)

If you remember only one thing I am saying here, please remember that God doesn't need your help—He needs only your obedience to keep your expectation alive. He's the one who made the promises to you in the first place and He's the one who's going to fulfill them. Let hope arise. Let faith grow. And keep expecting God to move at the speed of the supernatural. When you least expect it, God will fulfill His promises and answer all your prayers.

DON'T BE SHOCKED WHEN GOD "SUDDENLY" SHOWS UP

When our expectations are finally fulfilled, we are often found with our mouths hanging open in sheer amazement. Why? Usually, our sense of expectation has dwindled without us realizing it. Doubts have crept in and so we are shocked when what happens exceeds our earlier expectations.

While he was in prison, the apostle Peter could have felt impatient for the fulfillment of God's promises. *"But the church was earnestly praying to God for him"* (Acts 12:5). When God "finally" moved, it came as a shock. Peter hardly believed what was happening!

> *The night before Herod was to bring him to trial, Peter was sleeping between two soldiers, bound with two chains, and sentries stood guard at the entrance. Suddenly an angel of the Lord appeared and a light shone in the cell. He struck Peter on the side and woke him up. "Quick, get up!" he said, and the chains fell off Peter's wrists. Then the angel said to him, "Put on your clothes and sandals." And Peter did so. "Wrap your cloak around you and follow me," the angel told him. Peter followed him out of the prison, but he had no idea that what the angel was doing was really happening; he thought he was seeing a vision. They passed the first and second guards and came to the iron gate leading to the city. It opened for them by itself, and they went through it. When they had walked the length of one street, suddenly the angel left him.* (Acts 12:6–10)

Talk about a supernatural encounter! Peter was asleep the night before his trial. Worry and fear would probably have kept most of us awake, but not Peter. He was snoozing away when the angel appeared to him. The angel supernaturally set him free from his chains and opened the doors of the prison so Peter could walk out a free man.

Peter didn't believe his angelic escort out of prison was real, but he must have known the Lord would take care of him somehow. Otherwise, he surely wouldn't have slept so soundly while awaiting trial.

> *Then Peter came to himself and said, "Now I know without a doubt that the Lord has sent his angel and rescued me from Herod's clutches and from everything the Jewish people were hoping would happen." When this had dawned on him, he went to the house of Mary the mother of John, also called Mark, where many people had gathered and were praying. Peter knocked at the outer entrance, and a servant named Rhoda came to answer the door. When she recognized Peter's voice, she was so overjoyed she ran back without opening it and exclaimed, "Peter is at the door!" "You're out of your*

mind," they told her. *When she kept insisting that it was so, they said, "It must be his angel."*   (Acts 12:11–15)

While Peter was in prison, his friends and loved ones prayed like crazy. They were interceding for his release from prison. They were praying intensely and fervently, with great faith. And they were gathered in prayer when Peter knocked on the door. They had probably been praying with expectation, but I doubt it was for what they were about to witness.

IF YOU AREN'T EXPECTING VICTORY, YOU PROBABLY WON'T RECEIVE IT.

They were praying and standing in faith, and God still managed to amaze them. They couldn't comprehend the fact that Peter was knocking at their door. They were expecting God to work a miracle, but they weren't expecting a prison break. God suddenly moved at supernatural speed and they concluded it was Peter's angel knocking at the door.

Poor Peter! He kept knocking until they finally let him in. God often uses the shock factor for His own glory.

When you refuse to let anything diminish your sense of expectation while you're awaiting the fulfillment of God's promises, you will see the shocking, supernatural works of God on your behalf.

Many are the plans in a person's heart, but it is the LORD's purpose that prevails.   (Proverbs 19:21)

God knows His awesome plan for your life and His purposes for your circumstances. He wants you to know His plan, too, so that you can keep expectation alive. If you refuse to get distracted from your expectation of big things, God will deliver those things in His perfect timing.

God's timing is rarely immediate, but it often comes suddenly. *"When the **set time** had fully come, God sent his Son"* (Galatians 4:4).

Suddenly, the "set time" arrives. Suddenly, your prayers are answered. Suddenly, the promises of God are fulfilled.

Disappointed dreams and unmet expectations can be discouraging and depressing. These are only two of the reasons the devil loves to steal your expectation. If you aren't expecting victory, you probably won't receive it. If you aren't expecting to make it, you may not. Don't allow the devil to talk you into laying down your expectation and surrendering to his lies about your future. Your future is bright; your supernatural manifestation of the promises of God is just ahead. Keep hanging on to the God of hope and He will shower you with limitless blessings.

PART IV:

DISCOVER TRUE LIMITLESS LIVING

17

COMPONENTS OF CONSECRATED LIVING

We talked earlier about the importance of being separated from the world and consecrated to the things of God. The truth is, no dream, however beautiful, and no "land," however great, can truly satisfy us unless we're living a life that's centered on an intimate relationship with our heavenly Father.

In this chapter, I'd like us to explore some of the aspects of such a life, so we can develop and nurture the relationship that satisfies far better than any earthly achievement or material conquest.

A POWERFUL PRAYER LIFE

In order to experience the limitless life God has designed for us, we must devote ourselves to prayer, as we are exhorted to do. (See Colossians 4:2.) Prayer keeps us focused, alert, and sensitive to the guidance and revelation of the Holy Spirit. When we live our lives separated from the things of the world, we set the stage for regular times of prayer, intercession, and worship with the Lord.

During these times, the Holy Spirit reveals to us the condition of our hearts and the reality of our motives. We must go to the place of prayer daily for a "spiritual checkup." That way, when we veer off course, the Holy Spirit will work a needed realignment in us as we spend time in His presence—praying, reading, and meditating on the Scriptures, and worshipping God. But if we neglect to spend time in the Lord's presence through prayer, we are prone to drift off course and slowly slip away or backslide from the place where we need to be in God.

Let's stop merely going through the motions, and let's develop a powerful prayer life. Prayer is a vital element in keeping us focused on the things that are really important—the pursuit of our call and the advancement of God's kingdom.

The Lord told me years ago that if the enemy could distract me from prayer, he could distract me from my purpose and call. The enemy comes in sudden and sneaky ways to steal our focus and usurp our priority of prayer.

We have this charge from the apostle Paul: *"Be joyful in hope, patient in affliction, faithful in prayer"* (Romans 12:12).

To maintain a powerful prayer life, we must be faithful in prayer. We need to pray even when we don't feel like it. Tired, busy, emotionally drained—regardless of our state or circumstances, if we are self-controlled, we stay focused in prayer anyway.

Fasting, when paired with prayer, builds faithfulness because it forces us to submit the desire of our flesh to the commitment of our spirit-man. I am a big advocate of the practice of fasting. Fasting doesn't move God; fasting moves our flesh out of the way so we can hear His voice.

God is always trying to speak to us, but we are often so busy listening to our flesh—"I'm craving chocolate"; "I'm tired"; "I want pizza"—that we can't hear the still, small voice of the Holy Spirit. (See 1 Kings 19:12 KJV.) The voice of the flesh grows in volume, becoming louder and louder, the more we give in to it. The voice of the Holy Spirit, in turn, gets softer and softer in our lives. Whatever we feed becomes the stronger force. If we keep feeding our flesh its every desire, our flesh becomes the dominant voice over our spirit-man. If we feed our spirit-man by maintaining a powerful prayer life—marked by regular meditation on God's Word and heartfelt worship of Him—then our spirit becomes the stronger voice. We need to stay hidden in God's presence and focused on His voice above any other.

Paul wrote, *"Pray in the Spirit on all occasions with all kinds of prayers and requests. With this in mind, be alert and always keep on praying for all the Lord's people"* (Ephesians 6:18). When we are faithful to pray in the Spirit, it enables us to discern what is going on in the spiritual realm and keeps the fire of God burning in our lives. We are then equipped to remain alert.

> *Be alert and of sober mind. Your enemy the devil prowls around like a roaring lion looking for someone to devour.* (1 Peter 5:8)

The days and times in which we live are perilous. We need spiritual discernment as never before. Stay alert and keep on praying. Listen for the voice of the Holy Spirit and obey whatever He tells you. It will save your life and your soul.

We are urged to *"pray continually"* (1 Thessalonians 5:17). The King James translation of that verse is, *"Pray without ceasing."* Pray constantly, without stopping, and pray in the Spirit. The Holy Spirit prays for us when we don't know what to say. (See Romans 8:26–27.) That becomes true of us when we have been baptized in the Holy Spirit, with the evidence of speaking in tongues.

BAPTISM IN THE HOLY SPIRIT

When I first got saved, the idea of being baptized with the Holy Spirit freaked me out. I thought people who spoke in tongues were extremely weird. Anything unfamiliar can seem scary. Now, having been baptized in the Holy Spirit, I realize that all the things I did before I got saved are actually the weird and scary stuff.

We need all three members of the Trinity—God the Father, God the Son, and God the Holy Spirit. The Person of the Holy Spirit is the power of God on this earth to fulfill the will of the Father.

The first instance of people being baptized in the Holy Spirit is recorded in the book of Acts. The apostles were gathered together on the day of Pentecost, and this is what happened:

> *Suddenly a sound like the blowing of a violent wind came from heaven and filled the whole house where they were sitting. They saw what seemed to be tongues of fire that separated and came to rest on each of them. All of them were filled with the Holy Spirit and began to speak in other tongues as the Spirit enabled them.* (Acts 2:2–4)

A UNIVERSAL GIFT

The baptism of the Holy Spirit is not a gift for a select few. It's for every person who calls on the name of the Lord and surrenders his or her life to Him. The apostle Peter exhorted the believers of his day to be baptized in the Holy Spirit, saying:

> *Repent and be baptized, every one of you, in the name of Jesus Christ for the forgiveness of your sins. And you will receive the gift of the Holy Spirit. The promise is for you and your children and for all who are far off—for all whom the Lord our God will call.*
>
> (Acts 2:38–39)

The only requirements for being baptized in the Holy Spirit are getting saved and surrendering your life to the Lord.

Gifts are freely given and freely received. If you haven't yet received the gift of the Holy Spirit, ask the Lord to fill you to overflowing with His Spirit. The Holy Spirit desires to fellowship with you. Welcome the Person of the Holy Spirit into your life today!

WAIT PATIENTLY FOR THE GIFT

On one occasion, while [Jesus] was eating with [the disciples], he gave them this command: "Do not leave Jerusalem, but wait for the gift my Father promised, which you have heard me speak about. For John baptized with water, but in a few days you will be baptized with the Holy Spirit." (Acts 1:4–5)

When I was seeking the baptism of the Holy Spirit, I had to learn to wait for God to fill me. It wasn't easy because I wasn't very patient back then. I can remember getting discouraged and feeling I wasn't a "good enough" Christian because I hadn't yet received the gift.

Don't be impatient and give up on God as you await the gift of the Holy Spirit. Ask the Lord right now to baptize you in the Holy Spirit and then yield your tongue to Him.

ASK THE LORD TO BAPTIZE YOU IN THE HOLY SPIRIT AND THEN YIELD YOUR TONGUE TO HIM.

Be patient and keep on seeking the Lord to fill you. If you desire something strongly enough, you go for it, even if you have to wait a little longer than you would prefer. Don't give up; keep waiting and expecting in His presence. Don't make it harder than it is. Remember, it's a gift that Father God wants to give you. Don't "overthink" it like I did, only receive. Let the Holy Spirit speak through you in the prayer language that He wants to release through you today. It's biblical. It isn't weird, strange, or demonic.

John the Baptist told those he was baptizing, *"I baptize you with water for repentance. But after me comes one who is more powerful than I, whose sandals I am not worthy to carry. He will baptize you with the Holy Spirit and fire"* (Matthew 3:11).

It's the fire of God in our lives, through the baptism of the Holy Spirit, that burns out sin and compromise. The fire of God helps us to stay separate from the world and consecrated to the things of God. Welcome the fire of the Holy Ghost today. Don't stop seeking His presence until you are filled to overflowing.

SATURATION WITH THE LORD'S PRESENCE

When you are consecrated to the Lord, you are saturated with His presence. Countless people live life saturated in offense, sin, bitterness, and other self-destructive attitudes and habits. But the Lord wants us to be saturated with the glory of God.

Saturate means "to fill completely with something that permeates or pervades." When we are completely saturated in God's presence, we are like food that has been marinated in seasoning and dressing prior to being grilled, so when it is cooked, it tastes amazing. God wants us to be separated, consecrated, and saturated—"marinated" in His presence. That way, we are completely permeated with the nature of God, and we reflect that nature, or "flavor," in all that we say and do.

CLEAN HANDS AND A PURE HEART

Whenever we are expecting company, we clean our house and we strive to maintain that cleanliness. I don't know about you, but I'm expecting company. I'm expecting a visitation of the Holy Spirit in my life every day. I'm expecting Jesus to return to this earth at any time. I'm expecting company, so I keep my spiritual house clean.

The psalmist says, *"The one who has clean hands and a pure heart... will receive blessing from the LORD and vindication from God their Savior"* (Psalm 24:4–5). By having clean hands (acting with righteousness) and a pure heart (maintaining a proper attitude), we keep our spiritual house clean and ready for the best company: visitations of the Holy Spirit.

There's no limit to the Holy Spirit visitations that Father God wants you to experience. Expect company daily and keep your spiritual house clean. This requires us to keep our mouths shut and our hearts right. No matter what anyone else may say or do, we should resist the natural inclination to defend ourselves. Instead, we should turn the other cheek, as Jesus taught us to do. (See Matthew 5:39.) If we keep our hands clean and our hearts pure, we will receive blessings from the Lord. He will defend us and vindicate us.

Vindicate means "to free from allegation or blame; to provide justification or defense for; to protect from attach or encroachment." God is the only defense we will ever need. He will clear us of false accusations, uphold our cause, and defend us when others oppose our righteous ways.

Don't get in God's way by trying to defend yourself, and above all, do not seek revenge.

> *Do not take revenge, my dear friends, but leave room for God's wrath, for it is written: "It is mine to avenge; I will repay," says the Lord.* (Romans 12:19)

Your upright character and your ever-faithful God are your first line of defense. Get out of the way, and let God be God.

Declare the Word of God daily over yourself and your heart attitude so you may keep your spiritual house clean. The following two Scriptures are a couple of my favorites. I speak them out loud over myself regularly to make sure I'm found with a clean house—pure hands and a clean heart—whenever the Holy Spirit comes to call.

> *May these words of my mouth and this meditation of my heart be pleasing in your sight, LORD, my Rock and my Redeemer.* (Psalm 19:14)

> *Do not let any unwholesome talk come out of your mouths, but only what is helpful for building others up according to their needs, that*

it may benefit those who listen. And do not grieve the Holy Spirit of God, with whom you were sealed for the day of redemption.

(Ephesians 4:29–30)

Remember, there's no limit to the Holy-Spirit visitation that God wants you to experience. Put out the welcome mat and usher Him in with clean hands and a pure heart.

18

LOVE WITHOUT LIMIT

One thing that God definitely wants us to experience and give without limit is love. Paul wrote, *"And now these three remain: faith, hope and love. But the greatest of these is love"* (1 Corinthians 13:13) and *"For the entire law is fulfilled in keeping this one command: 'Love your neighbor as yourself'"* (Galatians 5:14). Jesus taught us that by loving the Lord our God and loving our neighbor as ourselves, we fulfill all the law. In other words, as long as we're loving well, we're living right.

WHAT IS LOVE?

We should desire to excel in the most important quality of all: love. What exactly is love—and what is it not? Most of us grew up thinking love was just one of many emotions that we experience in life. But we find a detailed definition in the thirteenth chapter of the first letter to the Corinthians. I find that the *Amplified Bible, Classic Edition* translation is particularly helpful in shedding light on the true definition of love.

This passage describes the heart attitude and daily actions of someone who is walking in love. Although these verses present a challenge that would take longer than a lifetime to perfect, it is what we should strive for daily. Next to salvation, our walk in love with the Lord and those around us are the most important things. After all, God is love.

> *Love endures long and is patient and kind; love never is envious nor boils over with jealousy, is not boastful or vainglorious, does not display itself haughtily. It is not conceited (arrogant and inflated with pride); it is not rude (unmannerly) and does not act unbecomingly. Love (God's love in us) does not insist on its own rights or its own way, for it is not self-seeking; it is not touchy or fretful or resentful; it takes no account of the evil done to it [it pays no attention to a suffered wrong]. It does not rejoice at injustice and unrighteousness, but rejoices when right and truth prevail. Love bears up under anything and everything that comes, is ever ready to believe the best of every person, its hopes are fadeless under all circumstances, and it endures everything [without weakening]. Love never fails [never fades out or becomes obsolete or comes to an end.]* (1 Corinthians 13:4–8 AMPC)

We shouldn't allow our priorities to get out of order. We can't afford to overlook the most important thing in life in our pursuit to get to something less important. We need to desire love more than anything else, for love is *"the most excellent way"* (1 Corinthians 12:31). Without love, we are nothing and we gain nothing. (See 1 Corinthians 13:1–3.)

LOVE GIVES

> *For God so loved the world that he gave his one and only Son, that whoever believes in him shall not perish but have eternal life.*
>
> (John 3:16)

Love *gives*! God so loved each one of us that He gave His only Son for us. That's huge! That's what love does—it gives. Love offers pardon and forgiveness when someone has been hurt and wronged. Love gives grace, kindness, compassion, and material blessings to those in need. When we truly love God and other people, we give.

LOVE PUTS OTHERS FIRST

Love is patient and endures long. Love is kind in words, attitudes, and nonverbal gestures. Love is never jealous or envious; thus, when we are walking in love, we rejoice when others are blessed. Because of love, instead of harboring a spirit of envy or covetousness, we are able to say, "Me, too, Lord. I know I'm next in line for my miracle!" In other words, we get excited for others when they receive their blessing and we know God will do the same for us because we are secure in His love for us.

Love *"keeps no record of wrongs"* (1 Corinthians 13:5). We often remember every wrongdoing that others have committed against us. If only we had that kind of memory for committing the Scriptures to heart! Stop memorizing and meditating on all the wrongs done to you and start memorizing and meditating on the Word of God. It will change your life.

WHEN WE ARE WALKING IN LOVE, WE REJOICE WHEN OTHERS ARE BLESSED.

Love does not boast; it is not vainglorious. *Boast* is defined as "to puff oneself up in speech" or "to speak of or assert with excessive pride." When we boast or speak in a prideful spirit, our actions and words do not show love to those listening to us. Instead, it may cause them to feel bad or inferior.

God's Word says it is *never* wise to compare ourselves with others.

We do not dare to classify or compare ourselves with some who commend themselves. When they measure themselves by themselves and compare themselves with themselves, they are not wise.

(2 Corinthians 10:12)

God's law of individuality has made each of us different and unique, but all equally wonderful. When we compare ourselves with someone else, we come out feeling either superior or inferior—and neither of these feelings brings glory to the Father. When we feel superior, we stand a good chance of stepping into pride, maybe even spiritual pride. When we feel inferior, we are apt to buy the lie that we're incapable or inadequate and we shrink back from stepping forward in faith to take the land.

A LIFE OF LIMITLESS LOVE

The only thing we should ever compare ourselves to is God's Word. Let's ask ourselves this question on a regular basis: *Do my life, my actions, my words, and my thoughts line up with God's Word? How about my heart attitude?*

God's Word reflects to us who we really are. When we regard ourselves in light of Scripture, we see a true reflection of our true identity. God's Word reveals to us what is motivated by our soul and what is motivated by our spirit. It judges our thoughts and the attitudes of our hearts, and the Holy Spirit reveals the truth to us. (See Hebrews 4:12.)

As we compare ourselves to the Word of God and evaluate ourselves in light of His desire for the direction of our lives, we can yield to the leading of the Holy Spirit and allow Him to make any necessary changes in us. But when we compare ourselves with others, we operate in the flesh, trying to be like others rather than like God.

Who are you trying to please as you endeavor to take the land? Are you trying to please other people? Your flesh? Or God and God alone?

PROMOTE LOVE, NOT DISCORD

Our utmost desire should be to love and promote love in everything we say and do. God's Word tells us, *"Whoever would foster love covers over* an offense, but whoever repeats the matter separates close friends" (Proverbs 17:9). Is your life promoting love? Or are your actions and attitude promoting offense? Are you jumping on the phone, telling everyone how badly so-and-so treated you? If that's the case, you'd better take a step back and regroup.

Let your life promote love and don't allow your mouth to cause division. It doesn't matter what someone else might have done to hurt you; your divine Defense Attorney has got you covered! Running your mouth by repeating the matter does not promote love, nor does it benefit anyone, yourself included.

When we "cover over" an offense, we are actually promoting love. But when we hold on to bitterness, anger, resentment, and so forth, we promote division and strain.

God wants us to promote love in our relationships and our communities. Doing so effectively will require us to rely on the power of the Holy Spirit working through us, which is just another reason why each of us needs the baptism of the Holy Spirit! The Holy Spirit makes and shapes us into the image of God. If you are like me, there needs to be a whole lot of shaping going on every day.

LOVE OTHERS AS YOURSELF

Speaking of the relationship between love and obedience, Jesus said, "My command is this: Love each other as I have loved you. Greater love has no one than this: to lay down one's life for one's friends" (John 15:12–13). As we follow the Lord's command to take the land, we must remember to love.

When we are in an all-out quest to conquer the land, let's not trample other people. Let's not run over, devour, or speak against others. Those ways are sure to hinder our anointing, grieve the Holy Spirit, and waste precious time and energy. Paul wrote, "If you bite and devour each other, watch out or you will be destroyed by each other" (Galatians 5:15). As we go forth to take the land, we must remember that those around us who are working for the Lord are not our competitors. We should view one another as business partners working together for the same CEO—the King of Kings and Lord of Lords. If we speak against a brother or sister in Christ, we "devour" that person with our tongue. As a result, we ourselves sustain the most damage.

Father God commands us to take the land, but He also commands us to love one another. How is your walk in love? If you are walking all over people with your words, you aren't walking in love, so no matter how much land you take, it amounts to nothing in the eyes of the Lord.

LOVE BY THE POWER OF GOD

Regarding the importance of loving one another, the apostle John wrote:

Dear friends, let us love one another, for love comes from God. Everyone who loves has been born of God and knows God. Whoever does not love does not know God, because God is love.

(1 John 4:7–8)

In order for us to walk in real love, the power and presence of God must be operating in our lives. God is love and when God lives in us through the indwelling of His Holy Spirit, we take on the nature of God, thus walking in love.

Love is one of the fruits of the Spirit. (See Galatians 5:22–23.) Fruit is grown, unlike spiritual gifts, which are given. (See 1 Corinthians 12.) We have to purposefully cultivate the fruit of love in our lives and actively develop our love walk on a regular basis. We can't pretend we are walking in love; we must put on love by clothing ourselves with this important fruit of the Spirit and allowing the Holy Spirit to work His love into us.

KEEP YOUR LOVE TANK FULL

God wants our "love tank" to be filled up every day. He wants us to know how much He loves us, every day, in every situation. He also wants us to experience His love as expressed to us by others.

How do you receive love from others? It's important for us to function on a full tank. If you are a giver, like me, you have to be careful not to allow "takers" to take, take, take, and never give back. Healthy relationships involve a balance of give and take. It's unhealthy to remain in relationship with people who don't treat you right.

> DON'T BE A "TAKER" YOURSELF AND DON'T ALLOW "TAKERS" TO DRAIN YOU.

Don't be a "taker" yourself and don't allow "takers" to drain you. You need "love tank fill-ups," too. If not, you can't take the land the way God intended for you to do.

MAKE GOD YOUR FIRST LOVE

I know your deeds, your hard work and your perseverance. I know that you cannot tolerate wicked people, that you have tested those who claim to be apostles but are not, and have found them false. You have persevered and have endured hardships for my name, and have not grown weary. Yet I hold this against you: You have forsaken the love you had at first. (Revelation 2:2–4)

The above passage, part of a letter from God to the church at Ephesus, was written because the people there were no longer as hungry for God and the things of God as they had once been. They were not as saturated with God's presence; they had strayed from their first love, the Lord.

Imagine the Lord Himself saying to you today what He said to the church in Ephesus: "I know all that you are doing for Me. I know all your hard work and perseverance for Me. I know how you have taken a stand against wicked people and those presenting a false image of themselves." Wouldn't that make you feel good? It's great when people notice our hard work and perseverance through trials and tribulations, especially if we are still persevering through problem after problem, trial after trial.

How much more gratifying would it be to have the Lord Himself notice and give you a pat on the back?

His next words, however, are sobering. *"But I have this complaint against you. You don't love me or each other as you did at first!"* (Revelation 2:4 NLT). For the church at Ephesus, that statement must have come as a shock. They probably thought they were getting straight A's on their "report card" until they reached that part of the letter.

They had forsaken their first love. They still had God in their lives, they still worked hard and persevered for His purposes, yet He no longer held the number one position in their hearts. There were other things and people they loved more than Him. They had lost the love they once had for the Lord and one another.

Ouch! That statement must've hurt. The truth often hurts, but we must face it and deal with it. Examine your heart today. Have you forsaken your first love?

When you are "in love," you glow, you radiate—you "share the love," so to speak. Everything about you reflects that love. And that's how we ought to be in our love for the Lord.

Speaking to the church at Ephesus, God went on to say, *"Consider how far you have fallen! Repent and do the things you did at first. If you do not repent, I will come to you and remove your lampstand from its place"* (Revelation 2:5).

If you have fallen away from the place where you were when you first got saved, repent today and resume doing the things you did at first. Remember how fired up you were for God when you first got saved? Remember how "crazy" you used to act when you fell in love for the first time? You had a love-struck gaze in your eyes. You would stay up all night talking to your "special someone." You would think about your loved one all day long and you'd wear a goofy grin the whole time. Well, as I always say, "There ain't no man like my Jesus!"

Return to your first love today. Let Jesus have your whole heart. Love Him more than anything and anyone else.

And then, the love of God in your heart will overflow to those all around you—even those who get on your nerves, those who have hurt or rejected you, and those whose company you don't always enjoy. Have you ever considered the possibility that they may just feel the same way about you? Either way, the Bible requires us to love everyone with the love of the Lord if we want to live a life that pleases our heavenly Father. As Jesus commanded us, *"Love your enemies and pray for those who persecute you, that you may be children of your Father in heaven"* (Matthew 5:44–45).

We are challenged to be victorious in the battle against evil and overcome the tendency to drift away from our first love. God's Word tells us, *"To the one who is victorious, I will give the right to eat from the tree of life, which is in the paradise of God"* (Revelation 2:7). Give God first place in your heart and allow His love to overflow from you to others. In this dark and despairing world, be a "glow-in-the-dark" Christian, illumined by the eternal love of God as you live a consecrated life for Him.

19

THE HOLY SPIRIT—CORNERSTONE OF LIMITLESS LIVING

In order to go all the way and cross over into a life of limitless living, we must tap into the limitless realm of God's glory. There is no limit to the Holy-Spirit visitation that God wants to release in your life and through your life. If we stop limiting the power and presence of God in our lives and yield to the Holy Spirit as He moves upon and within us, we will experience limitless living in the fullest sense of the term.

During a weekend conference where I was speaking, the Lord compelled me to share a statement I had never heard before and will never forget: "Yield to the manifestation of the visitation, and then you will receive the full impartation." After the Lord spoke this statement into my spirit, He showed me two illustrations of its truth from my own life. As you will see, it is imperative that we yield to the Holy Spirit and surrender our expectations of how and when He will visit us. Only then will we fully receive His power and presence—a gift of priceless value and no limits.

First, God reminded me of the time when my daughter was about three years old. I had been a single mother for almost as many years, since my husband had left when Destiny was just a few weeks old. I was still dealing with the pain of a broken marriage and all of the overwhelming emotions and challenges of being a single mom. On this particular occasion, I was attending a ministers' conference at a large church in Florida and I had chosen a seat in the front row. There were television cameras all around, zooming in for some close-up shots during the message given by Bishop T. D. Jakes.

I couldn't even scratch my nose without the whole world watching, so I felt disinclined to do anything but smile and stay focused on the message. I don't remember what Bishop Jakes was speaking on that night, but whatever the topic was, it struck a nerve in my heart. It took everything I had in me not to burst into tears and have a total meltdown, right there in the first row. Had I yielded, my crying would not have been subtle; tears and a runny nose would have sent competing streaks down my face.

I was grieving the loss of my marriage and the loss of my dream at the time. I was overwhelmed by just about everything happening in my life and ministry at that point. But I refused to embarrass myself that night. As the service continued, I bit my lip, held my tongue, and did everything I could think of to avoid crying. In my heart, I told the Lord, *I will cry when I get back to my hotel room tonight.*

Have you ever told the Lord what you will and will not do? Have you ever told the Lord how you want the Holy Spirit to move on you and in your life? That's exactly what I did that night, and it didn't go so well!

When I got back to my hotel room, I knew I needed a release through tears. I sat down on the bed and said to the Lord, "Okay, I'm ready to cry now." But I couldn't have cried even if my life had depended on it. I couldn't do anything. I just sat there.

The Lord taught me that night that I had better yield to the Holy Spirit above all—surrendering my feelings, preferences, pride, and so forth—if I want to tap into all that He has for me.

YIELD TO THE MANIFESTATION

The Holy Spirit manifests Himself to us in countless different ways. We can't presume to tell the Lord how and when we want the Holy Spirit to come upon us. Remember, the Holy Spirit is in control, not us!

> THE HOLY SPIRIT MANIFESTS HIMSELF TO US IN COUNTLESS DIFFERENT WAYS.

Sometimes, the Holy Spirit manifests Himself through our tears. When the Holy Spirit comes upon me, I often begin to weep gently. Other times, I sob deeply while tears rush down my face. At other times, the Holy Spirit manifests Himself to me by causing my body to shake or my hands to tremble. Sometimes, I feel the fire of God come upon me in the form of an overwhelming urge to run. And still other times, the visitation of His presence manifests in such a way that I can't even stand up, let alone move.

When we yield to the Holy Spirit's visitations, however they may manifest, we can receive the total impartation that the Lord wants us to receive. Often, in order to yield to the manifestation, we must "turn off" our natural minds, lest we think, *This looks silly*, or *How embarrassing*, and thereby close ourselves off to the Holy Spirit. Are we more interested in how we appear to others or in receiving the impartation the Father is trying to give us?

Yes, Father God wants to give us a heavenly "download" of Holy-Ghost power. We must yield to the manifestation of His visitations in order to receive the total impartation of His power.

Earlier this year, I was at a conference, seated (once again) in the front row. There weren't any TV cameras, but the Holy Spirit came upon me at a time that didn't seem very "convenient." The night before, many people had been laid out in the Spirit; personally, I had felt the presence of the Lord very strongly and God spoke to me, yet the manifestation of the Holy Spirit's visitation didn't knock me down or do anything dramatic.

The next night was a different story. The presence of God was extremely strong in the service, but everyone was still standing—everyone except for me, that is. Out of the blue, the power of the Holy Spirit came upon me and knocked me off my feet. I fell to the floor, and my head whipped backward between two chairs. As I lay there—half sitting, half lying down—my mind began to think, *You look pretty stupid.*

I immediately took my natural thoughts captive, bringing them under obedience to the Lord so I could continue to yield to the manifestation of His visitation in my life. (See 2 Corinthians 10:5.) I knew this yielding was necessary if I wanted to receive His total impartation.

I sometimes see people immediately jump up after the Holy Spirit has knocked them down. I've learned that if the Holy Spirit knocks me down, it's for a reason. He wants my undivided attention so He might speak to me, instruct me, and impart to me His power and wisdom. In this case, He showed me that a particular season of my ministry was complete.

We must determine to always yield to the manifestation of the Holy Spirit's visitation, so we will always receive the total impartation. Let's not limit His power and presence in our lives.

TIME WITH THE SPIRIT

When you are caught up in prayer, you lose track of time. When you are caught up in time, you lose track of prayer! Where are you today? In order to go all the way and take all the land—in order to live without limits—we must surrender our time and commit to a vibrant prayer life.

I have noticed that in the different seasons of my life, the Lord has required different things of me, according to the nature of the season. For years, the Lord wanted me to get up at four o'clock every morning and spend three hours studying His Word and praying. Why so early? Well, it was the only option for spending quality time with the Lord before my hectic day of ministry and "single-mommyhood" started!

During a recent conference in California, the Lord whispered to my heart, "I want you to start getting up at four a.m. for prayer again." I have learned that when I respond with immediate obedience, the Lord's grace will meet me right there. The next day, I woke up at four in the morning and the glory of God fell! This pattern continued for a week. Then, one morning at four, I felt as if a truck had hit me. The follow-ing morning, I was so tired from traveling that I felt like a wet noodle sleepwalking at four. But I hung in there and by a quarter after four, supernatural strength from above kicked in. The glory of God filled my room and the Father started telling me all manner of things He wanted me to know!

How has Father God been challenging you in your prayer schedule? Whatever He prompts you to do, you'll find it's best if you obey.

THE BENEFITS OF BEING INDWELLED BY THE HOLY SPIRIT

When it comes to limitless living, no lifestyle can compare with the joy, power, and peace of being indwelled by the Holy Spirit. When you have the Holy Spirit living inside you, nothing else really matters. Even the highest of human achievements fails to fulfill us like God's Spirit, as we dwell in His presence and soak up His Word.

Psalm 91 does a beautiful job outlining some of the benefits of being indwelled by God's Spirit. Read though it right now, then go on to explore some of those benefits in greater detail as I unpack them for you. Unlimited blessings and benefits, for now and eternity, are ours when we make the Lord Almighty our dwelling place.

Whoever dwells in the shelter of the Most High will rest in the shadow of the Almighty. I will say of the LORD, "He is my refuge and my fortress, my God, in whom I trust." Surely he will save you from the fowler's snare and from the deadly pestilence. He will cover you with his feathers, and under his wings you will find refuge; his faithfulness will be your shield and rampart. You will not fear the terror of night, nor the arrow that flies by day, nor the pestilence that stalks in the darkness, nor the plague that destroys at midday. A thousand may fall at your side, ten thousand at your right hand, but it will not come near you. You will only observe with your eyes and see the punishment of the wicked. If you say, "The LORD is my refuge," and you make the Most High your dwelling, no harm will overtake you, no disaster will come near your tent. For he will command his angels concerning you to guard you in all your ways; they will lift you up in their hands, so that you will not strike your foot against a stone. You will tread on the lion and the cobra; you will trample the great lion and the serpent. "Because he loves me," says the LORD, "I will rescue him; I will protect him, for he acknowledges my name. He will call on me, and I will answer him; I will be with him in trouble, I will deliver him and honor him. With long life I will satisfy him and show him my salvation." (Psalm 91:1–16)

PROTECTION

When we dwell in the presence of the Lord, we are in the shelter of the Most High. There's no other shelter like it. And that place of shelter belongs to us. *Shelter* is defined as "something that covers or affords protection." When we are walking with the Most High God, He's got us covered, He protects us and defends us.

Psalm 91 says we will "rest" in the shadow of the Almighty. Now, that's a picture of limitless living! What comfort there is in knowing we can rest because God is covering, protecting, and defending us. There's no earthly protection like that available at any price.

The Lord assures us, *"No weapon forged against you will prevail, and you will refute every tongue that accuses you. This is the heritage of the servants of the LORD, and this is their vindication from me"* (Isaiah 54:17).

Even when other people, including the devil himself, try to "forge" weapons against us, those weapons will be proven false. God is our defense!

When God says, *"You will refute every tongue that accuses you,"* that doesn't mean we will provide a verbal defense for ourselves. It doesn't mean we will jump in and start telling it "like it is." Our character is what will refute all false accusations. No legitimate charges can be brought against God's servants who are living right and dwelling in the secret place.

PEACE

One definition of *rest* is "peace of mind or spirit." When we dwell in the secret place of the Lord Almighty, peace and fear can't coexist in our hearts and minds. We can be at peace, face life with ease, and lead lives of refreshment, even in the midst of challenging situations.

Psalm 23 is a proclamation of the peace that can be ours in Christ Jesus. In it, the psalmist says, *"Even though I walk through the darkest valley, I will fear no evil, for you are with me; your rod and your staff, they comfort me"* (Psalm 23:4). We can rest and be at peace even when we are walking through the darkest of valleys, because the Lord has us covered. We can be refreshed at times and in situations where other people would be fearful, stressed out, and overwhelmed.

We are way too blessed to be stressed. There's no limit to the peace and refreshment that can be ours when we dwell in God's presence.

JOY

When I read Psalm 91 and other Scriptures that outline the features of a limitless life lived in God's presence, it brings me unspeakable joy. Rejoicing rises up in my heart and spirit when I reflect on all the benefits that are mine when I am indwelled by the Holy Spirit.

Joy itself is yet another benefit of dwelling in the presence of the Almighty. We had better guard our joy, for it's a great source of strength. (See Nehemiah 8:10.) God gives us a joy that cannot be taken away unless we willingly surrender it.

I'm reminded of a time when Destiny was about two years old. She got into trouble, so I put her in her playpen for time-out. Even as I told her how long she would have to stay in there, she looked right at me, smiled broadly, and declared, "I'm not going to let you steal my joy, Mommy!"

> GOD GIVES US A JOY THAT CANNOT BE TAKEN AWAY UNLESS WE WILLINGLY SURRENDER IT.

After I turned around and walked away, I burst out laughing.

Don't allow the enemy to steal your joy. Don't allow people or situations to rob you of the joy of the Lord. Remain in God's presence and allow Him to fill you with His all-surpassing joy.

True joy is not dependent upon our circumstances; it's dependent upon our relationship with the Lord. If we haven't been dwelling in the secret place of the Most High, then we can't expect to be joyful. Our source of joy is the very presence of the Lord.

WISDOM AND DISCERNMENT

God's wisdom is a stabilizing force in our lives and it's available to us without limit, if we only ask for and receive it.

> *If any of you lacks wisdom, you should ask God, who gives generously to all without finding fault, and it will be given to you. But when you ask, you must believe and not doubt, because the one who doubts is like a wave of the sea, blown and tossed by the wind. That person should not expect to receive anything from the Lord. Such a person is double-minded and unstable in all they do.*
>
> (James 1:5–8)

God is very generous with His wisdom—we need only ask Him for it. And He grants us His wisdom without finding fault with us. He doesn't say, "Gosh, here comes Danette again, bugging Me for more wisdom." No, He gives generously to all who ask. As we dwell with the

Lord in the secret place, we receive His wisdom upon request. But when we have received it, we must believe what the Lord has told us and not doubt.

God's wisdom enables us to exercise discernment in our decisions, whether daily choices or momentous judgment calls. A valuable lesson I have learned is to trust my God-given discernment.

When we are in the presence of the Lord, we hear His voice and discern His leading. But when we come out of that secret place and go about our daily lives, if we aren't careful, we can begin to doubt what the Lord has said.

I can remember the first time I received a word of knowledge from the Lord. I was in church, praying at the altar, and by the time I returned to my seat, I had already begun to doubt. The Lord spoke to me through that incident and showed me how the enemy comes immediately to steal the Word. (See Luke 8:12.) If we begin to doubt, we become double-minded. And if we maintain such a mind-set—with an uncertain faith that wavers from day to day—it begins to affect other areas of our lives and we become unstable in all we do.

However, when we dwell in the secret place, we can remain stable and fixed under the shadow of the Almighty. When the enemy realizes we are not movable, he'll move on to mess with someone else.

BE A CARRIER OF THE GLORY

Whatever it is that we have been called to do, the Lord wants to carry us across the threshold into the new realm. Let His glory carry you as you determine in your heart to go all the way, and set out to fulfill every plan and purpose the Lord has planned for you.

You can take all of the land and live life for Christ without limits. There's no limitation to the Holy Spirit visitation in your life unless you place a limit on it. For a carrier of the glory who's determined to go all the way, a limitless lifestyle for the glory of God is yours for the asking.

20

LEAD OTHERS INTO THE LAND

God has called every one of us to be a leader. From corporate CEOs to stay-at-home moms, all of us are leaders in some capacity. And our potential as leaders is determined by the extent of our training and preparation.

Our individual processes of training and preparation will differ according to the various leadership positions God has called us to. A religious leader's season of "get ready" will look different from a political leader's.

Regardless of their nature, all leadership positions are important; no single position is greater than another. The key is our obedience to being trained and equipped to fulfill the responsibilities of the position

238 *LIMITLESS THINKING, LIMITLESS LIVING*

to which God has called us. Remember, all parts of the body are of equal importance. (See 1 Corinthians 12:18–19.)

One leader's season of "get ready" may last much longer than another's. I can remember thinking, during my own season of "get ready," *What in the world is taking so long?* That season seemed to last twenty years! What's important is not the length of our season, but our successful completion of it. It takes more time to lay the foundation for a thirty-story high-rise than for a two-story home. Remember, God is the Builder, the Master Architect. Don't mess with the Master! Don't try to rearrange His blueprints. Father God knows what He's doing. You and I must simply submit to the building process as we "get ready" for our crossover.

ARISE AND LEAD WHEN GOD SUMMONS YOU

After the death of Moses, the Lord spoke to Joshua and told him he was to arise and begin to lead the people of Israel. Joshua and the children of Israel were given thirty days to grieve the death of Moses, but after that, they were challenged to get up and move forward.

Sometimes, when the Lord tells us it's time to arise and lead, we question His choice and His timing. But God always fulfills His will in His timing. He does things in such a way that He gets all the glory.

WHEN WE ARE SO WEAK THAT WE CAN'T EVEN MOVE, GOD CARRIES US.

My husband left me when our daughter was a newborn and I went through a very difficult time grieving the loss of my marriage. A year later, the Lord told me to get up out of my mess and go do what I was called to do. When I heard this message, I felt more emotionally and spiritually drained than ever before. It was the worst storm I had ever been through and God was telling me to get up and lead. I thought, *Are You serious, God?*

Yes, God was serious! And as I stepped forward in faith, God held my hand, giving me the grace to move on and up in my faith. When I took my eyes off myself and kept my focus on the Lord, following His lead, I was amazed at the supernatural grace and strength that God extended to me.

On the days when we can't even hold our own head up, so to speak, God supernaturally props us up. When we are so weak that we can't even move, God carries us. It's during these times that God gets all the glory.

Joshua was tired and weary after grieving the loss of Moses, yet the Lord challenged him to move on and move up. God told him, *"Be strong and courageous, because you will lead these people to inherit the land I swore to their ancestors to give them"* (Joshua 1:6). I believe the Lord is challenging you in the same way today.

Webster's New World College Dictionary supplies the following definitions of *strong*: "physically powerful...morally powerful...powerfully made, built, or constituted; tough; strong; durable...; hard to capture; able to resist and endure attack." I love the definition "able to resist and endure attack." The truth is, we are engaged in spiritual warfare on a daily basis, and we must be able to resist the attacks of the enemy with our strength in the Lord. That way, we can step into the positions of leadership that God has called us to fulfill.

STEP OUT IN OBEDIENCE

Years ago, the Lord said to me, "I never have a hiring freeze on. I'm just looking for qualified applicants." You are God's chosen vessel. You have been selected by God for a specific purpose. Many are called, but few are chosen. (See Matthew 22:14.) Why? Because only a few will obey the Holy Spirit's leading. God wants you to step out in obedience and be strong and courageous as you pay the price to lead His people.

Some of the people you are called to lead don't want to be led. Some of them aren't yet walking with the Lord. That's why God needs us all to report for duty and walk in obedience to His every instruction.

Press past how you feel. Press past what you think and what you think you want, and obey the leading of the Holy Spirit. You will always be glad you did!

Webster's New World College Dictionary defines *courage* as "the attitude of facing and dealing with anything recognized as dangerous, difficult, or painful, instead of withdrawing from it; quality of being fearless or brave; valor." When faced with difficult and challenging situations, we would often prefer to withdraw or retreat. But when we are courageous, we face each challenge head-on with the power of the Holy Spirit. We don't rely on our own abilities, but we depend on God's love and strength to get us through. Will you be strong and courageous today? Will you get up and lead, as the Holy Spirit empowers you?

GET UP AND LEAD

Father God has called each and every one of us to be a leader. If you are a stay-at-home mom, you are leading your children. Whether you work as a cashier or a business owner, in a warehouse or an office, you are called to lead others by your attitude, example, and witness for the Lord. Maybe you are called to lead in a full-time ministry position. Whatever the place and position that God has put you in today, you are called to lead right where you are. The question is, will you get up and lead?

This is my charge to you today:

Arise [from the depression and prostration in which circumstances have kept you—rise to a new life]! Shine (be radiant with the glory of the Lord), for your light has come, and the glory of the Lord has risen upon you! (Isaiah 60:1 AMPC)

Father God is saying to all of us, "Arise! All rise and prepare to lead!" In order for you to lead, you must first get up. Sometimes, God calls us to move on and move up at times when we feel weak and weary. But when we make the choice to arise from our circumstances—even those that have brought us to a place of depression and discouragement—we can begin to shine and radiate with the glory of God. God wants you to arise to a new life and refuse to allow your circumstances to keep you down any longer.

You may have been down and out for a long time. Father God is saying to you today that it's time to get up and out of the slump. It's time to get out of the state of grieving. It's time to arise and shine!

DO NOT DWELL ON THE PAST

To answer the call to lead, you must first arise. You must first get up out of your "mess" and release the old things in your life so you may embrace all of the new things the Lord has for you.

Joshua had to release the old season of his existence—the season in which Moses was the leader and Joshua was his assistant. We will always have our memories of the past, but we must be obedient to move on and move up when the Holy Spirit tells us to do so.

The Lord loves doing new things. He's a fan of moving forward. He tells us, *"Forget the former things; do not dwell on the past. See, I am doing a new thing! Now it springs up; do you not perceive it? I am making a way in the wilderness and streams in the wasteland"* (Isaiah 43:18–19). We "forget" the former things when we release our past to the Lord.

Release all of your past—the good, the bad, and the ugly—so you can embrace the glorious future the Lord has for you. The great "I Am" is doing a new thing in you today. He's not the great "I will be" or the great "I was"—He is the Great "I Am." (See Exodus 3:14; John 8:58.) He's an ever-present help in times of trouble—right now, right where you are. (See Psalm 46:1.)

There comes a time when we must stop talking about our past, whether it was lousy or lovely, and must start talking about our glorious future in the Lord. The Lord is trying to bring forth a brand-new season in your life, so stop hanging on to the past in your mind, your words, and your thoughts.

242 LIMITLESS THINKING, LIMITLESS LIVING

You can't change the past or undo anything that has already happened, but you *can* change the future by stepping into the new, as Paul speaks about doing. (See Philippians 3:13–14.) You can't "fix" things or people from the past, but you can "fix" your mind on things above and focus on your glorious future. (See Colossians 3:1– 4.) Let Father God bring you into the new season.

God is *"doing a new thing,"* but we must see it or recognize that this is so. It's springing up now. Stop dragging your feet because it's coming forth right now! Get out of your comfort zone and move into your potential zone.

You have to perceive it. You have to wrap your mind around it. It will require having a new mind in Christ for you to perceive what God is about to do through you.

> *Do not conform to the pattern of this world, but be transformed by the renewing of your mind. Then you will be able to test and approve what God's will is—his good, pleasing and perfect will.*
>
> (Romans 12:2)

Get your soul—that which you want, think, and feel—under the control of your spirit so you can perceive God's next move for you. Forget the former things, stop dwelling on the past, and arise as you step into your new season.

STRENGTH TO GET UP

We have to get good at "getting up." Life's circumstances will knock us down from time to time. Other people will bowl us over. But by the power of the Holy Spirit, we can get good at getting up. If we don't get up once we have been knocked down, we won't be able to lead.

You can't take someone to a place if you haven't first been there yourself—and this is particularly true of your walk with the Lord. But the Lord will give you supernatural strength to get up. Call on His name and stay determined to move on and move up.

God *"gives power to the faint and weary, and to him who has no might He increases strength [causing it to multiply and making it to abound]"* (Isaiah 40:29 AMPC). When we take a step of faith to get up and lead, God causes our strength to increase and multiply. That's a great deal! But there's more:

> But those who wait for the Lord [who expect, look for, and hope in Him] shall change and renew their strength and power; they shall lift their wings and mount up [close to God] as eagles [mount up to the sun]; they shall run and not be weary, they shall walk and not faint or become tired. (Isaiah 40:31 AMPC)

If you let Him, God will renew your strength by exchanging your weakness for His might. As we keep our hope in the Lord, He supernaturally recharges our spiritual, emotional, and mental batteries with strength and power to move on and move up.

It was God, and God alone, who brought me through the challenging years of raising my daughter as a single mother. Year after year, through challenging circumstances, God gave me supernatural strength and power to get up and lead.

Don't ever give up; always get up. Keep moving on and moving up. Put your hope in God alone. Trust in Him and look expectantly to Him in all things, for all things. You will never be disappointed.

IF YOU LET HIM, GOD WILL RENEW YOUR STRENGTH BY EXCHANGING YOUR WEAKNESS FOR HIS MIGHT.

God says to us, "See, I have refined you, though not as silver; I have tested you in the furnace of affliction" (Isaiah 48:10). God sometimes allows us to pass through certain trials in order to make us into the leaders He has called us to be. He often tests us in the fiery trials of affliction. When we have passed through them, we can more effectively lead others who are passing through trials of their own.

LEAD OTHERS TO FREEDOM

When we are confident of our freedom in Christ—freedom from sin, guilt, man-made traditions, and so forth—our example will set others free. Once we can say with the psalmist, "*I will walk about in freedom, for I have sought out your precepts*" (Psalm 119:45), we can model freedom in worship, prayer, and other spiritual disciplines so others might be set free from the bondage of meaningless religious rituals, firmly ingrained fears, and the tormenting lies of the enemy.

When we live in freedom, we are free to lead others through our prayers for them and by our witness to them. Remember, our lives speak much louder than our words.

Jesus said, "*If the Son sets you free, you will be free indeed*" (John 8:36). Let the Lord set you free so you can lead others in freedom and *to* freedom. Remember, you can never lead anyone to a place where yourself have never been.

GREAT LEADERS ARE LED BY THE LORD

How do we know where to lead those who follow us and look to our example? We lead them in the footsteps of the Holy Spirit, of course! That's just what Joshua did. He led the Israelites to the presence of the Lord, where we find the truest freedom this side of heaven.

After three days the officers went throughout the camp, giving orders to the people: "When you see the ark of the covenant of the LORD *your God, and the Levitical priests carrying it, you are to move out from your positions and follow it."* (Joshua 3:2–3)

Joshua instructed the people to follow the ark of the covenant, which represented the presence of the Lord. We must follow the presence of the Lord, or the leading of the Holy Spirit, every moment of every day. That way, when we lead others, we always draw them into the presence of God.

We can successfully lead others by following the presence of the Lord day by day, moment by moment. When we desire His presence more than anything else, we can keep the fire of God burning in our lives. When that fire is burning, we desire His presence. And when we desire His presence, we delight to follow His leading.

GREAT LEADERS DESIRE THE LORD ABOVE ANYTHING ELSE

God's Word says, *"Take delight in the* LORD, *and he will give you the desires of your heart"* (Psalm 37:4). When we take delight in the Lord, we long for His presence and desire His will more than anything else. And when we take delight in the Lord and abide in His presence, the desires of our hearts begin to line up with the will of God for us. God then grants us the desires of our hearts because we have allowed ourselves to be led by Him. All of a sudden, we find ourselves desiring the very things God knows are His best for us.

When the Lord and His presence are our strongest desires, we can be confident that we're leading others along the right path because we know we're pursuing God's plans for us.

GREAT LEADERS LEAD HOLY LIVES

Joshua told the priests to carry the ark of the covenant ahead of the people. (See Joshua 3:6.) Joshua led the priests—the leaders of his people—and the priests led the people with the presence of the Lord. In the same way that you can't take anyone to a place where you've never been, you can't take anyone higher than the place where you are.

Let's say a church worship leader is living in sin. He won't be able to take the congregation into the Holy of Holies because he isn't abiding in the Holy of Holies. Leaders can lead others only as high as the level where they themselves live.

Don't allow anyone to lead you if he isn't living a holy, consecrated life. But if you must stop following him, please don't judge him. It's a fine line. That's why you need to live in the presence of the Lord. *"When he, the Spirit of truth, comes, he will guide you into all the truth"* (John 16:13). He will show you the truth about yourself and the situations around you.

Again, true freedom is found in God's presence. As Paul wrote, *"Now the Lord is the Spirit, and where the Spirit of the Lord is, there is freedom"* (2 Corinthians 3:17). Freedom in worship, freedom in the mind, freedom from emotional wounds and baggage—all this and more comes from being in God's presence and soaking in His Word of truth. God wants you to be free to go to the "high places" of praise. He wants you to be free to enter the Holy of Holies.

Living a holy life is true freedom, while living in sin and compromise is true bondage. *"Through Jesus the forgiveness of sins is proclaimed to you. Through him everyone who believes is set free from every sin"* (Acts 13:38–39). True freedom is not about doing what you want to do when you want to do it. It comes from obeying the Word of God and living according to God's principles. Leading a holy life, or being Christ-like, enables us to experience freedom in its truest sense, discover limitless living at its best, and set others free to do the same.

GREAT LEADERS USHER OTHERS INTO THE KINGDOM

God wants to use us, His servant-leaders, to produce limitless fruit for the kingdom of heaven. The truth is, the only things we can take with us to heaven are the souls we have led to salvation. No earthly achievement matters as much as leading others to Christ and winning souls for the kingdom.

Real limitless living is allowing the God of the universe to use you to win souls and change lives for eternity. Few experiences are more rewarding. The Word tells us, *"The fruit of the righteous is a tree of life, and he who wins souls is wise"* (Proverbs 11:30 NKJV). Let your life become a tree of great fruit for the kingdom—the fruit of souls saved and set on a path for heaven.

BE YOURSELF AS YOU LEAD

When David decided to fight the giant Goliath, King Saul told him, *"You are not able to go out against this Philistine and fight him; you are only a young man, and he has been a warrior from his youth"* (1 Samuel 17:33).

Once David told the king about his experience fighting off and even killing lions and bears, Saul agreed to let him fight Goliath, but still insisted on imposing his "advice," telling David what he ought to wear. *"Then Saul dressed David in his own tunic. He put a coat of armor on him and a bronze helmet on his head"* (1 Samuel 17:38).

IT'S CRUCIAL THAT YOU BE BOLD AND CONFIDENT THAT GOD IS GOING TO USE YOU.

Sometimes, other people will try to tell you how to do something and they don't even realize what they are doing. I've had loved ones who have never preached a message in their life try to tell me how to preach—even when I'd been doing it for twenty years. Anyone can offer "expert" advice from a well-meaning heart, yet even our best intentions don't necessarily mean our advice is needed, wanted, or helpful.

It may be that no one else is confident or convinced of God's ability to do a certain work through you, or to use you to lead His people. Even so, it's crucial that you be bold and confident that God is going to use you. When you believe it, you can see it. When you believe big, you can see big. Although no one else had confidence in him, David saw nothing but big victory. And big victory was his outcome! But he had to stay true to himself in order to achieve it.

> *David fastened on his sword over [Saul's] tunic and tried walking around…"I cannot go in these," he said to Saul, "because I am not used to them." So he took them off. Then he took his staff in his hand, chose five smooth stones from the stream, put them in the pouch of his shepherd's bag and, with his sling in his hand, approached the Philistine.* (1 Samuel 17:39–40)

David was open to Saul's advice because David was a teachable, humble servant. Yet David was confident enough to speak up and say, "This isn't going to work!" He knew he would succeed only if he went into battle as himself. If he had tried to be someone else by using another's armor and weapons, the outcome could have been totally different. It would have been really hard to fight wearing armor that he wasn't used to. More important was the fact that God had anointed David when he was confident enough to be himself.

I started preaching and traveling as an evangelist at the age of twenty-one. I can remember trying to be like others I admired. It came as a revelation to me when God said, "You will be anointed when you are just yourself!" Sure enough, when I was preaching as myself, the glory would fall. When I tried to preach like someone else I respected, it would fall flat. Thank the Lord I was a quick learner because it's really embarrassing when you are trying to be someone else and there's no anointing on the service.

Years later, I started my own television show. Early on, when filming, I would just "let it rip." I preached on television the same way I preached at my revival services. Then the "experts" weighed in, instructing me on how to minister differently on television. Trust me, they got very detailed in their "how to" descriptions.

One so-called expert told me I needed to be like Terry Meeuwsen from *The 700 Club*. I love Terry Meeuwsen; she is an amazing woman of God. Since I respected her so much, I gave it a try. It didn't take long for me to figure out that trying to do my television program as she did hers was not going to work at all. It was flat and boring. The anointing was absent.

I'm not wired like Terry Meeuwsen. I am an evangelist in the body of Christ. I'm loud, with a built-in microphone, and I'm high energy. I have a hard time sitting still while performing the most mundane of tasks, so I definitely can't sit still while I'm preaching the Word of God. It's as if I have fire inside like the prophet Jeremiah, who said, *"His word is in my heart like a fire, a fire shut up in my bones"* (Jeremiah 20:9). Imagine trying to sit still when there's a fire in your bones. That's how it felt for me. And it looked just as awkward on camera.

But when I cut loose and felt free to be myself, the anointing would fall and viewers at home would be set free. The anointing of the Holy Spirit sets people free from bondage.

Who are you trying to be today? Can you say, "I'm free to be me"? "I'm free to lead others while still being true to myself, to the way God has made me"? Or are you still trying to fit into someone else's mold? Just be yourself as you lead others to take the land in their lives!

CONCLUSION:
ONCE YOU'VE CROSSED OVER

When God is in the middle of our situation, as He was with the Israelites in the middle of the Jordan River, miracles happen. Whenever it's time for us to transition to a new level, God supernaturally parts the waters (our circumstances) so we may cross to the other side. But what happens next? What are we supposed to do once we have crossed over? How should we proceed once we've taken the land?

We are supposed to encourage the next generation to think big, expect big, ask big, and do big things, too. Our testimony of God's faithfulness and power at work on our behalf will encourage others to adopt a mind-set of limitless thinking for themselves, so they can walk in the freedom and unfettered potential that come from a life without limits in Christ.

DON'T BE COMPLACENT IN THE PROMISED LAND

God wants each of us to cross over and take the land in every area of our lives. Then after we have stretched the limits and defeated the giants, He wants us to help others experience the same blessings and victories in their own lives.

Joshua expressed a similar desire for the children of Israel:

Remember the command that Moses the servant of the LORD *gave you after he said, "The* LORD *your God will give you rest by giving you this land." Your wives, your children and your livestock may stay in the land that Moses gave you east of the Jordan, but all your fighting men, ready for battle, must cross over ahead of your fellow Israelites. You are to **help them until the** LORD **gives them rest**, as he has done for you, **and until they too have taken possession of the land the** LORD **your God is giving them**. After that, you may go back and occupy your own land, which Moses the servant of the* LORD *gave you east of the Jordan toward the sunrise.*

(Joshua 1:13–15)

Joshua was explaining to the Israelites that after they took their own land, they had to help everyone else do the same. They could not merely sit back, relax, and enjoy all that God had done for them. No, they had to help each other. Only then could they occupy and enjoy their own land.

Once we have expanded our thinking, enlarged our expectations, and received big blessings from the hand of God, let's not get so comfortable and complacent in that place of blessing that we forget about those around us who are still waiting to cross over into their own promised land.

Are you sitting around enjoying the "land blessings" God has given you? Or are you actively helping others to achieve their own crossover?

Remember, God will turn your test into your testimony, if you'll only allow Him to do so. Just make yourself available and be willing to help others cross over and take their own land.

PASS ALONG THE LEGACY OF LIMITLESS THINKING

So Joshua called together the twelve men he had appointed from the Israelites, one from each tribe, and said to them, "Go over before the ark of the LORD your God into the middle of the Jordan. Each of you is to take up a stone on his shoulder, according to the number of the tribes of the Israelites, to serve as a sign among you. In the future, when your children ask you, 'What do these stones mean?' tell them that the flow of the Jordan was cut off before the ark of the covenant of the LORD. When it crossed the Jordan, the waters of the Jordan were cut off. These stones are to be a memorial to the people of Israel forever." (Joshua 4:4–7)

Joshua wanted to make sure that the next generation maintained the limitless thinking that God had worked into the hearts and lives of their parents' generation.

Each generation ought to grow from glory to glory and evidence an expansion in their mind-set from that of the previous generation. Each generation should do greater things for the Lord than the one before. And in order to do all that, they must be thinking big!

> THE WAY THAT WE THINK, WHETHER BIG OR SMALL, MAKES A PROFOUND AND LASTING IMPACT ON THOSE WE INFLUENCE.

What legacy will you leave for the next generation? What mind-set do you model for your children? The way that we think, whether big or small, makes a profound and lasting impact on those we influence, especially our own children.

As we choose to adopt an open mind-set of limitless thinking, the fruit that comes from our life will be without limit. Step into the supernatural and walk daily in the miraculous by removing the limits from your thinking. There's no limit to what God will do in you, through you, and for you. Just think big, ask big, and expect big from the One who can do immeasurably more than we can imagine.

ABOUT THE AUTHOR

Danette Joy Crawford is a powerful international evangelist, author, speaker, and TV host with a refreshing message of hope and encouragement. She is the founder and president of Danette Crawford Ministries, which aims to spread the gospel around the globe with its media endeavors. Its outreach arm, Joy Ministries Evangelistic Association, organizes inner-city work with over twenty different compassion programs. It offers more than a handout; it gives a "hand up" to those in need. Through educational and mentoring programs, it assists at-risk youth and low-income families. The ministry also has many programs for single mothers, including Cars for Moms and Back to Work programs. Homeless single mothers and children are provided transitional housing through the Father's House, which empowers single mothers to move forward after a difficult season of homelessness.

Danette's television program, *Hope for Today with Danette Crawford*, is broadcast weekly into over 250 million homes. She and her ministry have been featured on ABC, CBS, NBC, TCT, TBN, Dove Network, *The 700 Club, The Harvest Show, Paula White Today, 100 Huntley Street*, and other television shows and networks, as well as in numerous newspaper and magazine articles.

Danette is the author of several books, including *Don't Quit in the Pit; God, You've Got Mail; Total Turnaround; Pathway to the Palace*; and *The Standard Setters*. In everything she does, her goal is to see souls saved and lives changed. Danette holds a master's degree in counseling from Regent University. Her website is: www.DanetteCrawford.com.